In God's Image

In God's Image

a global Anabaptist family

Ray Dirks
foreword by Larry Miller

published in cooperation with
Mennonite Heritage Centre Gallery
and Mennonite World Conference

Herald Press
Waterloo, Ontario
Scottdale, Pennsylvania

**Herald
Press**

National Library of Canada Cataloguing in Publication
Dirks, Ray, 1955-
    In God's image : a global Anabaptist family / Ray Dirks.
Includes bibliographical references.
ISBN 0-8361-9254-0
    1. Anabaptists. 2. Anabaptists—Pictorial works. I. Title.
BX4931.3.D57 2003   305.6'43   C2003-902456-3

IN GOD'S IMAGE: A GLOBAL ANABAPTIST FAMILY
Copyright © 2003 by Herald Press, Waterloo, Ont. N2L 6H7.
    Published simultaneously in USA by
    Herald Press, Scottdale, Pa. 15683. All rights reserved
Canadiana Entry Number: C2003-902456-3
Library of Congress Control Number: 2003105352
International Standard Book Number: 0-8361-9254-0 (paperback)
                                     0-8361-9272-9 (hardback)
Printed in Canada
Cover photography by Ray Dirks
Book design by Ray Dirks
Edited by Larry Kehler
Foreword by Larry Miller
All other text and photographs by Ray Dirks unless otherwise noted
Printed by Friesens, Altona, Manitoba, Canada
Project of the Mennonite Heritage Centre Gallery, Winnipeg, Manitoba, Canada

10 09 08 07 06 05 04 03 10 9 8 7 6 5 4 3 2 1

To order or request information, please call
1-800-759-4447 (individuals); 1-800-245-7894 (trade).
Website: www.heraldpress.org

to Katie, Lauren and Alexa, and to mom and dad for allowing me to dream

Table of contents

In God's Image

a global Anabaptist family

17 countries

daily life photos & art

preface

After my first year of art school my wife Katie and I opted for travel rather than for me to return to Vancouver Community College's Art in Merchandising program. As a young boy I had read about Hiram Bingham and his discovery of the lost city of the Incas in Peru. The accompanying photo of Machu Picchu stayed with me. Thus in 1978, with little money but many dreams, we set out on a long, meandering journey to Machu Picchu. In the end, what most intrigued me were not the ancient ruins — undoubtedly one of the most spectacular historic sites in the world — but rather the ordinary people we passed along the way. I returned to Canada with a new desire to experience the lives of ordinary people in parts of the world foreign to my perceptions of what is "normal".

A few years in Kinshasa, Zaire (now Democratic Republic of Congo)

cemented my interest in common people from places not common to me. Upon leaving Kinshasa I was gripped by a passion to honor people from places in the world we tend to blanket with negative stereotypes. Both as an artist and as a curator my career steered towards a focus on ordinary people as created in the image of God, as equal in the eyes of God to whoever our world holds up as important. I have tried to do this by working with contemporary artists from Africa, Asia and Latin America, offering them opportunities to show us their people as people of dignity who are worthy of respect, revealing things which I as a foreigner to their cultures have not quite seen. I also attempt to place the respect I believe God demands of me for his human creations in my art, photography and writing. In exhibits I curate, in art I make, in words I string together, in photographs I take, I pray that the fact that we are all created in the image of God is always central.

This book comes out of a wish to celebrate the global Anabaptist faith family as it exists early in the 21st century. It includes a broader church introduction, written by Larry Miller of the Mennonite World Conference, alongside stories and photographs from the lives of ordinary church members from 17 participating countries. Art from each of these countries is also featured. Our wish is to portray every person in the book, regardless of country, church, gender, age or culture, as equal — as created in the image of God.

All countries with churches related to the Mennonite World Conference were notified of this project and were asked if they would like to take part. Including all countries or every conference in each participating country was not feasible. Those that responded favorably to our notification were given priority, keeping in mind that we needed a global balance that would properly reflect the makeup of the Anabaptist church. Participating countries were visited over a 21-month period ending in May 2003. Stories and photos were gathered. Art was purchased or donated for an exhibition that comes out of a broader project that includes this book. The project is based in the Mennonite Heritage Centre Gallery in Winnipeg, Canada.

The book is not meant to look like *National Geographic*. The photographs are not necessarily technically perfect. No filters or extra tricks were used. The purpose was to create an intimate, approachable, real snapshot of a global family. This is, in a way, a large family album. It is not about people who exist in filtered, beautiful photographs somewhere seemingly beyond our reality — people whom we can't get to know. At the related exhibition's opening at the National Gallery of Zimbabwe in Bulawayo one Zimbabwean observer said to me, "I feel like I have just taken a trip around the world visiting friends along the way." That is the reaction we desire, that readers have traveled the world meeting family.

I debated within myself for a long time about how personal the writing in this book should be. My wish was not to place myself at the center of it. My wish was to focus on the ordinary people I met in each country. At the same time it seemed to me that making the writing almost as if it came out of a personal journal would enhance the intimacy, emotion, immediacy and reality within the text and photos.

I am passionate about the people in this book. They, like you and I, are created in the image of God. As I traveled, as often as possible I stayed in the homes of ordinary church members, hoping to experience their daily lives as they do, and then to sympathetically pass on to the readers the gifts they offered me through their hospitality, love, faith and kindness.

I am also passionate about the art in this book. Visual artists are gifted by God to reveal special insights into cultures, thoughts, beauty, issues and emotions. For too long many churches have not recognized the talents of artists as coming from God. The art included here adds another layer to the book.

I have visited Machu Picchu in Peru. That journey changed me, switching my greatest interest to people. Since then I have visited India. But not the Taj Mahal. I stayed with the widow of a former pastor of 53 years in a small, anonymous village in Andhra Pradesh. I saw an old woman working quietly, diligently, with graciousness and humility to keep a small church community alive and relevant. That is more inspiring than the most beautiful, awesome edifices created by humans. My prayer is that the people in this book will feel properly and respectfully represented, and that you, the reader, will feel a passion for this wondrous global family rising from these pages, and that you will share in it.

Ray Dirks

Acknowledgment: Each chapter begins with country and church information. All country information was found through BBC, World Bank and infoplease.com. All church information courtesy Mennonite World Conference.

The United Nations Human Development Index (HDI) measures a country's achievements in terms of life expectancy, educational attainment and adjusted real income.

Abang Rahino photo, Indonesia

2003 Membership of Mennonite, Brethren in Christ and Related Churches
Membres
Membresía
Mitgliederzahl

127 851 Canada
Canada
Canada
Canadá
Kanada

323 329 United States
United States
Etats-Unis
Estados Unidos
Vereinigte Staaten

2 070 Cuba
Cuba
Cuba
Cuba
Kuba

731 Jamaica
Jamaica
Jamaïque
Jamaica
Jamaika

1 265 Haití
Haiti
Haïti
Haití
Haiti

4 626 República Dominicana
Dominican Republic
République Dominicaine
República Dominicana
Dominikanische Republik

540 Puerto Rico
Puerto Rico
Porto-Rico
Puerto Rico
Puerto Rico

130 Trinidad-Tobago
Trinidad and Tobago
Trinité et Tobago
Trinidad-Tobago
Trinidad und Tobago

19 688 México
Mexico
Mexique
México
Mexiko

3 575 Belize
Belize
Bélize
Belice
Belize

6 673 Guatemala
Guatemala
Guatémala
Guatemala
Guatemala

20 716 Honduras
Honduras
Honduras
Honduras
Honduras

535 El Salvador
El Salvador
Salvador
El Salvador
El Salvador

9 275 Nicaragua
Nicaragua
Nicaragua
Nicaragua
Nicaragua

2 719 Costa Rica
Costa Rica
Costa-Rica
Costa Rica
Costa Rica

750 Panamá
Panama
Panama
Panamá
Panama

704 Venezuela
Venezuela
Venézuela
Venezuela
Venezuela

2 910 Colombia
Colombia
Colombie
Colombia
Kolumbien

810 Ecuador
Ecuador
Equateur
Ecuador
Ecuador

515 Perú
Peru
Pérou
Perú
Peru

8 262 Brasil
Brazil
Brésil
Brasil
Brasilien

13 275 Bolivia
Bolivia
Bolivie
Bolivia
Bolivien

27 693 Paraguay
Paraguay
Paraguay
Paraguay
Paraguay

1 220 Uruguay
Uruguay
Uruguay
Uruguay
Uruguay

4 448 Argentina
Argentina
Argentine
Argentina
Argentinien

5 000 Commonwealth of Independent States
Commonwealth of Independent States
Communauté des Etats indépendants
Comunidad de Estados Independientes
Gemeinschaft unabhängiger Staaten
(Members in Kazakhstan, Kyrgyzstan, Russia, Ukra

112 United Kingdom
United Kingdom
Royaume Uni
Reino Unido
Vereinigtes Königreich

15 Eire
Ireland
Irlande
Irlanda
Irland

2 050 France
France
France
Francia
Frankreich

55 Portugal
Portugal
Portugal
Portugal
Portugal

160 España
Spain
Espagne
España
Spanien

11 000 Nederland
Netherlands
Pays-Bas
Países Bajos
Niederlande

35 Belgique
Belgium
Belgique
Bélgica
Belgien

110 Luxembourg
Luxembourg
Luxembourg
Luxemburgo
Luxemburg

300 Österreich
Austria
Autriche
Austria
Österreich

31 677 Deutschland
Germany
Allemagne
Alemania
Deutschland

2 500 Schweiz
Switzerland
Suisse
Suiza
Schweiz

25 000 members

o 1 000 members or less

Membership statistics indicate baptized members. Statistics include estimates. Listing on this map does not denote membership or participation in Mennonite World Conference.

Statistiques de membres baptisés, dont certaines sont approximatives et ne reflétant pas l'appartenance ou la participation à la Conférence Mennonite Mondiale.

Las estadísticas de membresía indican miembros bautizados, incluyendo algunos datos estimados. No todos los grupos que figuran este mapa son miembros activos del Congreso Mundial Menonita.

Die Mitgliederstatistik zeigt die getauften Glieder, enthält aber auch Schätzungen. Eine Darstellung auf dieser Karte bedeutet nicht die Mitgliedschaft oder Beteiligung bei der Mennonitischen Weltkonferenz.   Design by Julie Kauffman.

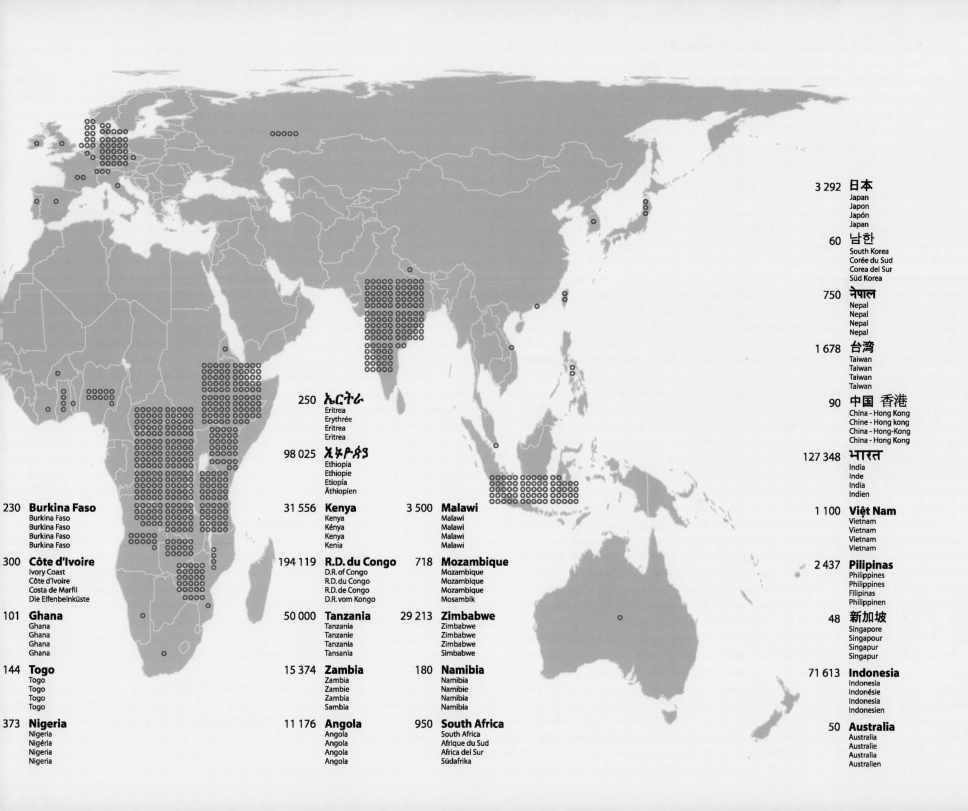

3 292 日本
Japan
Japon
Japón
Japan

60 남한
South Korea
Corée du Sud
Corea del Sur
Süd Korea

750 नेपाल
Nepal
Nepal
Nepal
Nepal

1 678 台湾
Taiwan
Taiwan
Taiwan
Taiwan

90 中国 香港
China - Hong Kong
Chine - Hong kong
China - Hong-Kong
China - Hong Kong

127 348 भारत
India
Inde
India
Indien

250 ኤርትራ
Eritrea
Erythrée
Eritrea
Eritrea

98 025 ኢትዮጵያ
Ethiopia
Ethiopie
Etiopía
Äthiopien

1 100 Việt Nam
Vietnam
Vietnam
Vietnam
Vietnam

2 437 Pilipinas
Philippines
Philippines
Filipinas
Philippinen

48 新加坡
Singapore
Singapour
Singapur
Singapur

71 613 Indonesia
Indonesia
Indonésie
Indonesia
Indonesien

50 Australia
Australia
Australie
Australia
Australien

230 Burkina Faso
Burkina Faso
Burkina Faso
Burkina Faso
Burkina Faso

300 Côte d'Ivoire
Ivory Coast
Côte d'Ivoire
Costa de Marfil
Die Elfenbeinküste

101 Ghana
Ghana
Ghana
Ghana
Ghana

144 Togo
Togo
Togo
Togo
Togo

373 Nigeria
Nigeria
Nigéria
Nigeria
Nigeria

31 556 Kenya
Kenya
Kénya
Kenya
Kenia

194 119 R.D. du Congo
D.R. of Congo
R.D. du Congo
R.D. de Congo
D.R. vom Congo

50 000 Tanzania
Tanzania
Tanzanie
Tanzania
Tansania

15 374 Zambia
Zambia
Zambie
Zambia
Sambia

11 176 Angola
Angola
Angola
Angola

3 500 Malawi
Malawi
Malawi
Malawi
Malawi

718 Mozambique
Mozambique
Mozambique
Mozambique
Mosambik

29 213 Zimbabwe
Zimbabwe
Zimbabwe
Zimbabwe
Simbabwe

180 Namibia
Namibia
Namibie
Namibia
Namibia

950 South Africa
South Africa
Afrique du Sud
Africa del Sur
Südafrika

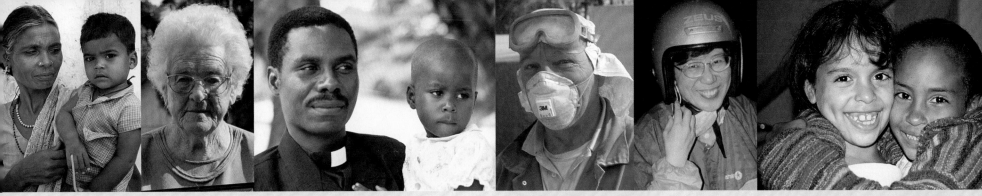

around the world in the Anabaptist family of faith [1]

baptist family of faith

Amidst all the war and pain of the 20th century, the time and space in which we live was radically redefined. Transportation and communications revolutions compressed the world into one basic unit and intensified our consciousness of it as a single place. This "global village" became the primary place for many spheres of human existence, shaping our daily lives in ways we hardly suspect.

In the church, too, a kind of globalization took place.[2] In 1910 a great world mission conference met in Edinburgh, Scotland. Nearly everyone present was European or North American. There were very few Asians and Latin Americans — and not a single African. In their deliberations, conference delegates divided the globe into two parts, the Christianized West and the non-Christianized rest. Indeed, at that time more than 80 percent of all Christians lived in Europe and North America.

But the situation changed radically in the next decades. Western missions, independent indigenous movements, and quickening population growth dramatically expanded the church in the global South. Today, less than 40 percent of the world's two billion Christians are European and North American. More than 61 percent live in Africa, Asia and Latin America. And by 2025, Africa and Latin America will be the most populous regions of the Christian world — with North America numerically the smallest.

In other words, during the most violent century in world history, the Christian population became authentically global. No longer primarily European in location and character, as it still was 100 years ago, the church is now found in nearly every country. The heartlands of Christianity are moving from the West and the North to the East and, especially, to the global South.

GOING GLOBAL, MOVING SOUTH

The 20th century demographic and cultural shift in the Anabaptist-related family was still more sweeping.[3] In 1900, 99 percent of the Anabaptist-related family lived in Europe (including Russia) and North America — and many could still converse with one another in German or some Germanic derivative. Today,

8

61 percent of us call Latin America, Asia or Africa home.

	Christians in 1900	% of Total	Christians in 2003	% of Total	Anabaptists in 1900	% of Total	Anabaptists in 2003	% of Total
Africa	8,756,000	2	360,059,000	18	100	0	452,209	35
Asia	25,081,000	5	349,413,000	18	2,400	1	208,155	16
Latin America	60,027,000	11	498,399,000	25	0	0	133,150	10
Europe	368,210,000	71	538,068,000	28	150,000	66	53,272	4
North America	59,570,000	11	217,387,000	11	75,000	33	451,180	35
Total	521,644,000	100	1,963,326,000	100	227,500	100	1,297,966	100

This globalization of the Anabaptist-related population began in earnest at the turn of the century. In 1850, we lived in no more than eight countries, all in the global North. But the years 1890-1917 saw a burst of activity as Mennonite or Brethren in Christ missionaries entered India, Zimbabwe, China, Nigeria, Zambia, Congo and Argentina (They had already gone to Indonesia in 1851.). By 1978 Mennonite or Brethren in Christ churches had been organized in 44 nations of Asia, Africa, Latin America, Europe, and North America. Today we live in at least 66 countries worldwide (see "2003 Membership of Mennonite, Brethren in Christ and Related Churches," pages 6 and 7).

In short, from early sixteenth century roots in several northern European groups, the Anabaptist branch of the Christian family has spread into over 100 cultures. Global membership now approaches 1.3 million baptized believers, representing a community of about two million people, speaking at least 75 languages and constituting more than 13,000 local churches in over 200 national conferences of churches. Most importantly for the future, the majority of us are African, Asian and Latin American. These are the people who will play the dominant role in determining what it means to live as Anabaptist Christians at the end of the 21st century.

Sadly, deepening economic disparity accompanies this global transformation. Most of

the numerical growth in the Anabaptist world, as in Christianity generally, is taking place among people who are financially poor. Wealth — and the education, health and long life expectancy that it buys — remains concentrated in the hands of North American and, to a much smaller degree, European family members.

	Percent of MWC Membership[4]	Percent of MWC Membership's Estimated Wealth[5]
Africa	43.26	0.85
Asia	20.44	2.13
Latin America	8.30	1.72
Europe	2.40	6.97
North America	25.59	88.33

Even apart from economics, of course, typical churches of the global South and those of the North look, sound and think quite differently when compared to one another. Not only are we "red, brown, yellow, black and white," but also our expressions of the faith are multicolored. Church services in Africa, Asia and Latin America tend to last longer and be more enthusiastic, more musical, more in tune with the immediacy of the supernatural, through prayer and healing, for example. An element of dancing or other physical movement is also more common in worship in churches of the global South than in typical European and North America congregations. The most significant difference, however, may be how the newer churches in the family are entirely at home in the cultural world of the Bible. Southern churches are naturally at ease with biblical descriptions of spiritual blessings and struggles, prophecies and visions. For many, the themes of poverty, suffering, oppression and exile are immediately relevant (just as they have been for numerous Anabaptist Christians from the sixteenth century onwards). These are people who spontaneously see in their own life situations the daily circumstances of those the Jesus of the Beatitudes calls "blessed."

So, do Anabaptists in the South and those in the North really have

anything in common? Can the older and younger parts of the family connect and stay connected? Or are we on the way to becoming two (or many more) fragmentary families — "an older fading northern variety, made of wealthy, secularized and post-modern people, and a southern variety which is poor but vibrant, exercising spiritual power, practicing personal faith and reaching out with evangelistic zeal?"[6]

Indeed, for some the globalization of the Anabaptist-related family has led to so much diversity of local identity that it makes no sense to speak of a worldwide family or, still less, of a family of faith. "Very little connects one place with the other; little do the people know of one another. A Mennonite Indian in the Chaco and a Mennonite businessman in Krefeld, a Mennonite woman in Tanzania and a Mennonite housewife in Siberia — worlds separate them. Perhaps they all refer back to a mutual confessional source, especially to their nominal patron Menno Simons of Witmarsum. But what they believe and how they believe separate them no less from each other than from Catholics, Lutherans and Mennonites in Europe and North America. The 'worldwide brotherhood' is an illusion [...]."[7]

For others, the variety resulting from the globalization of the family is the source of our prosperity and a call to sharing. "I think the first time I [an American] was struck by my great wealth was in Luanda, Angola, in 1999. It was a Sunday morning in November. I came before the congregation to give words of greeting, [...] I recall struggling to decide what words I should offer them — this group about whom I knew so little and with whom I obviously had so little in common. I knew nothing of their theology, as they knew nothing of mine. I knew nothing of their joys, their sufferings, or their daily lives. Yet these were people who understood themselves to be part of a family of which I, too, considered myself a part. How could this be? What did it mean? As I stood looking over all those beautifully different faces, I was overcome by one thought: What wealth! What incredible, lovely riches! And how terrible it would be not to be related to them! I felt weighted down with a kind of burden of gratitude, a sense that somehow, in ways I cannot understand, my connectedness to these people was both a fact and a wish, a statement of what is and what can be. It was like a clear, still voice that said, 'This is the path...follow it!'"[8]

SHARING CONVICTIONS, SHARING GIFTS

The diversity in which we now live articulates the alternative offered to us by the globalization of Anabaptist-related Christianity. Shall we live our lives as if the notion of a worldwide faith family is an illusion? Or shall we take as a basic operating principle the conviction that we are, in fact and in calling, a global family?

The member and associate churches of MWC[9] have made their choice: "Mennonite World Conference is called to be a communion (*Koinonia*) of Anabaptist-related churches linked to one another in a worldwide community of faith for fellowship, worship, service and witness."[10] The worldwide family of faith is not an illusion, or at least should not be. We desire connection, relationship, interdependence, common identity and action. The time has come to live not only as local and national churches but also as global community. We belong together. We will learn from one another. We will grow together. We will share convictions. We will share gifts.

What core convictions characterize the family today? Meeting in Bulawayo, Zimbabwe (August, 2003), MWC member and associate member church delegates asked that question and approved this brief statement of "shared con-victions" for testing with the churches worldwide during the next three years.

By the grace of God we seek to live and proclaim the good news of reconciliation in Jesus Christ. As part of the one body of Christ at all times and places, we hold the following to be central to our belief and practice:

1. God is known to us as Father, Son and Holy Spirit, the Creator who seeks to restore fallen humanity by calling a people to be faithful in fellowship, worship, service and witness.

2. Jesus is the Son of God who showed in his life and teaching how to be faithful, and through his cross and resurrection redeemed the world.

3. The church is a community of those whom God's Spirit calls to turn from sin, acknowledge Jesus Christ as Lord, receive baptism upon confession of faith, and follow Christ in life.

4. *The faith community, under Holy Spirit guidance, interprets the Bible in the light of Jesus Christ to discern God's will for our obedience.*

5. *The Spirit of Jesus empowers us to trust God in all areas of life so we become peacemakers who renounce violence, love our enemies, seek justice, and share our possessions with those in need.*

6. *The faith community gathers regularly to worship, to celebrate the Lord's Supper and to hear the Word of God in a spirit of mutual accountability.*

7. *We seek to live in the world without conforming to the powers of evil, witnessing to God's grace by serving others, caring for creation and inviting all people to know Jesus as Saviour and Lord.*

In these convictions we draw inspiration from Anabaptist forebearsers of the 16th century, who modeled radical discipleship to Jesus Christ. Walking in his name, by the power of the Holy Spirit, we confidently await Christ's return and the final fulfillment of God's kingdom.

Living as a global family "faithful in fellowship, worship, service and witness" means sharing gifts. Every member needs connections to every other member in order to be part of the body and to produce life abundantly. Giving to and receiving from one another what God first gave us binds us together while it implements God's intention for the world.

What gifts are found in the global family? MWC's Global Gift Sharing workshops reveal a great wealth of gifts and resources — particularly human resources — in Anabaptist-related churches everywhere (See the church profiles in the following pages for a few of the gifts highlighted by the Global Gift Sharing project.). These communities are made up of gifted human beings created in God's image; in this sense there is no such thing as a poor church anywhere in the global family. The gifts seem innumerable: gifts of creation, gifts of special skills, gifts of insight and inspiration, material gifts, relational gifts. The challenge for a global faith family is recognizing, developing and sharing such great wealth. A Congolese pastor put it this way: "In music, the notes of the scale are all needed to make an agreeable sound — one note on its own is not interesting. In the church, we have many gifts but often they are disorganized. Our different gifts are like different notes of music; they need to be arranged and put together in a harmonious way. The time has come for our community to put all our gifts together for the good of all."[11]

PART OF A BIGGER FAMILY

Yet, as only one member of the body of Christ created in the image of God, sharing convictions and sharing gifts merely in our own little family would be heretical. To live as a global Anabaptist family is to declare that we are but a small part of the worldwide Christian family. Dozens of other world churches seek to live as global Christian families. Each one seeks to be an expression of the divine impulsion toward Christian community. Each one can be an experience of the church universal, rendering the body of Christ more visible in the world. But each one of us does so incompletely and imperfectly. It is this knowledge that draws us to relationship with other Christian families of faith, sharing convictions and sharing gifts as fully as possible — so that there may be life abundant for the entire world.

Larry Miller, Mennonite World Conference

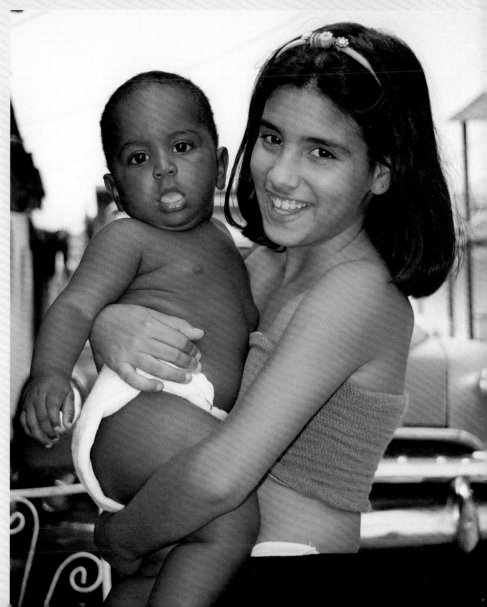

[1] Anabaptism was a sixteenth century reform movement with both significant diversity and a common core of faith and practice (C. Arnold Snyder, *From Anabaptist Seed: the Historical Core of Anabaptist-related Identity*, commissioned by Mennonite World Conference, Pandora Press, Kitchener, Ontario, Canada 1999). "Anabaptist" and "Anabaptism" have a variety of contemporary usages among groups that identify themselves as lineal or spiritual descendants of historic Anabaptists. (For these people, the terms have a positive ring even though they were initially used pejoratively by those who opposed the movement and still retain negative connotations in significant sectors of the Christian church.) In this book, "Anabaptist family" refers to the Mennonite, Brethren in Christ, and related churches identified in the *Mennonite & Brethren in Christ World Directory 2003* (Mennonite World Conference, Strasbourg, France) and, more specifically, to the member and associate member churches of Mennonite World Conference.

[2] World Christian statistics and predictions in this chapter come from David B. Barrett and Todd M. Johnson, especially their "Annual Statistical Table on Global Mission: 2003," *International Bulletin of Missionary Research* 27, January 2003, pp. 24 and 25.

[3] Anabaptist-related statistics for 1900 are based on estimates by John A. Lapp and Ed van Straten ("Mennonite World Conference 1925-2000: From Euro-American Conference to Worldwide Communion," *Mennonite Quarterly Review* 77, January 2003, p. 8), slightly revised, as well as Wilbert Shenk's estimates for 1911 (*By Faith They Went Out*, Institute of Mennonite Studies, Elkhart, Indiana, 2000, p. 94). Figures for 2003 come from the *Mennonite & Brethren in Christ World Directory 2003*.

[4] The continental percentages for "MWC membership" are different than the continental percentages for "Anabaptists in 2003" (see table, page 9) because about 1/5th of Anabaptist-related Christians do not belong to MWC member or associate member churches.

[5] Based on number of baptized members in national conference (source: *Mennonite & Brethren in Christ World Directory 2003*) and Gross Domestic Product per capita of the country (source: World Bank, *2003 World Development Indicators Database*).

[6] Nancy Heisey, "Anabaptist Heritage and Faithful Diversity," Schrag Lecture, Sider Institute for Anabaptist Studies, Grantham, Pennsylvania, 6 March 2003, p. 4.

[7] Hans-Jürgen Goertz, "From the edge to the center," in Dieter Götz Lichdi (editor), *Mennonite World Handbook: Mennonites in Global Witness*, Mennonite World Conference, Carol Stream, Illinois, USA, 1990, p. 287.

[8] Tim Lind, in Pakisa K. Tshimika and Tim Lind, *Sharing Gifts in the Global Family of Faith: One Church's Experiment*, published in cooperation with Mennonite World Conference by Good Books, Intercourse, Pennsylvania, 2003, p. 15 ff.

[9] Ninety-seven national conferences of churches in fifty-three countries are members or associate members of Mennonite World Conference.

[10] MWC vision statement, adopted in Bulawayo, Zimbabwe, August, 2003.

[11] Reported by Pakisa Tshimika and Tim Lind, *Sharing Gifts in the Global Family of Faith*, p. 59.

Democratic Republic of
Congo

surface area: 2,345,410 sq. km.
capital: Kinshasa
population: 52.7 million (2003)
language: French, Lingala, Kiswahili, Kikongo, Tshiluba
major religion: Catholic 50%, Protestant 20%, Kimbanguist 10%, Islam 10%; syncretistic and traditional, 10%
literacy: 72%
life expectancy: 41 (men), 43 (women)
annual income per capita: US $80

United Nations Human Development Index: 167 out of 175 countries (2003)

Mennonite World Conference
Member Churches

Name: Communauté des Eglises de Frères Mennonites au Congo
Local churches: 629
Members: 85,648

Name: Communauté Evangélique Mennonite
Local churches: 160
Members: 21,871

Name: Communauté Mennonite au Congo
Local churches: 531
Members: 86,600

Gift Highlights: Choirs, Bible schools, resources for cooperative mission efforts, animal traction program, joint service opportunities, Theological Education by Extension (TEE) and Bible school correspondence courses, peace/conflict resolution worker, appropriate technologies for women's enterprises

Democratic Republic of Congo

Kinshasa Kikwit Mbuji-Mayi
Tshikapa

(opposite) A newly ordained pastor's congregation escorts him home after his ordination service.

family stories

Released, the thankless thugs revisited the man and family they had already wronged. A victim who chose to forgive, a victim who felt as a Christian and a Mennonite he was called to forgive, had asked for no charges to be filed. He asked for the criminals to be released. The military men responsible for ransacking the pastor's home a week earlier returned after their release with reinforcements to the scene of their original crime.

Unfortunately, this retelling is fact not fiction. A happy ending was not to be. Pastor Nzelenga, a Mennonite Brethren minister in Kinshasa, was slain along with a son on the verge of graduating from high school. Stories of heroes do not always have happy endings. In 2003 a Mennonite Brethren pastor in Kinshasa, Democratic Republic of Congo (DR Congo), was murdered, martyred because he tried to do the right thing according to his Anabaptist convictions.

The husband and father of seven was given a funeral paid for by the state because he was also a chauffeur for the United Nations. The sanctuary was filled to overflowing. Testimonies, passion and frustration with the endemic violence in a tortured country split the air.

The DR Congo is a haunting, majestic country of giant rivers, thick jungle and endless savannah. It is a country with great natural resources — minerals, land, water, forests — and with boundless potential in God's earth and in God's people.

DR Congo struggles mightily within colonial boundaries combining more than 200 tribes in one country. King Leopold of Belgium set a savage example of colonialism at its worst. After the turmoil around independence, President Mobutu followed in Leopold's steps, making exploitation for his own gain his

only reason to rule. He was a friend of America and France, feted by President Reagan in Washington while listed as the most corrupt ruler on earth, allowing his corruption to continue without much attention in the West. Mobutu's pathetic last days, combined with the spillover from the genocide in Rwanda, the entering of the country by armies from various countries, old tribal hatreds coming to the fore as various groups fought for power and resources — whether real or meager — threw the huge Central African country into a horrid civil war that led to millions of deaths, more from disease than physical slaughter.

As the current government struggles for legitimacy and to right a potential African giant, the church continues to shine. Hope is found in the church. During a recent rebellion Mennonite citizens in the city of Kikwit organized peace volunteers to give food and shelter to soldiers going through the city. Soldiers, supposedly trained to protect the public, are often the main cause of chaos — from petty crime to murder — in DR Congo. The militia are feared and often unpredictable. Practicing what is written in Romans 12:17-18 led to Kikwit being spared from pillage. "If someone does evil to you, do not pay them back with evil. Try to do what all people consider to be good. Do everything possible, on your part, to live at peace with all people." The soldiers passed through the community without incident.

In spite of all its turbulence the DR Congo is not without joy. Visitors to most any church are welcomed as if they are royalty. Attending a service in the country is not to be forgotten. Troubles wash away, passion and pain are unleashed, support is searched for and found. The church is the center of music, thought, counsel and community in many, many instances.

CEFMC (Mennonite Brethren) Mbumbu in Kinshasa is famous for its music in a country full of churches known for the quality and enthusiasm of their choirs. An intangible artistic energy thrives in DR Congo. Whether in the visual arts, street style or in music, contemporary secular or Christian, this spirit is readily evident. It cannot really be explained. It must be experienced. Mbumbu, to borrow a Western term, rocks. Pastor Tshibi has been a musical leader in Mennonite Brethren circles for more than two decades. He is known and respected throughout the conference.

Churches can have many choirs. Mwanza Ngunza is a longtime member of a men's choir at Mbumbu. He says that the gift of the Congolese church is its music. It brings joy and hope to many in a suffering country, both to those who sing and those who listen.

Choirs tend to have names. The young men's choir at Mbumbu is "Choradi," worshippers of God. The ladies choir "Mwinda," light. Individuals can also present songs, often composed by themselves during the week

before as a response to a particular issue or concern. On a recent Sunday an old woman sang a song exhorting the youth to be faithful. "Bana, keba mpo na bizaleli na bino na mokili oyo." The congregation, including the youth to whom she sang, erupted with joy and affirmation after her self-composed song. The song was appreciated, and her compassion and concern were also acknowledged in the cheers.

Offering time is when the music is really unleashed as choruses run into and out of one another without a breath. There is no slowing down when the offering music builds. Spontaneous dancing is not unusual. Sometimes offerings are taken by passing the collection baskets along rows. Sometimes people exit their pews to place their offerings in baskets at the front of the sanctuary. Then women, men and youth may be separated into competing groups and each go up to give their offerings as a unit. In such lines the dancing sometimes looks choreographed, especially as the women sashay down the aisle, wrapped in layers of colorful Congolese cloth, a ribbon of beauty stepping and swooping elegantly, gracefully towards their designated basket.

Offerings can be channeled to a number of things. At the same service at Mbumbu where the old woman sang to the youth, three offerings were taken. One was for the speaker. He was given money to cover his transportation to and from the church and enough for about three meals. A second was for the regular church budget. A third was taken spontaneously at a different point in the service. It raised money for someone who was in the hospital. This offering did not end with the money being given. Two women and a man were appointed or volunteered on the spot to take the money to the sick person.

During the service Pastor Mambakila explained how the previous week's offering was used. It helped cover expenses for Pastor Tshinyama's funeral. Pastor Tshinyama passed away the Monday before. He was an important CEFMC pastor and taught many years at a Kinshasa theological school. He died of complications due to diabetes. He was the acting president of the CEFMC Pastors' Council. All the churches were asked to participate.

Whether to help ordinary members or to help cover the costs of a pastor's funeral the church is an important cog in Congo's suffering economy. It is a place where people can find solidarity and support in times of crisis and loss. Churches are places to feed the soul and the body. They have, in many ways, become the social welfare system in a country whose government has had difficulty working even at the most basic level in recent years.

Mwanza Ngunza and his wife Angélique Nsimba, while ordinary members of the congregation, are important cogs in the Mbumbu church. They married shortly after Mwanza graduated from the Kinshasa Vocational School in 1990.

Joy in a suffering country during congregational singing in Mbumbu church.

(above, below and opposite) Scenes from Mwanza Ngunza's and Angélique Nsimba's family and church life in Kinshasa.

Their family includes four children and, as in many African families, two other dependents — young relatives are living with them. Mwanza has participated in the church since he was a small boy. Angélique is a choir member and youth counselor in the church. Noting their exemplary lives, the church has asked Mwanza and Angélique to be mentors to a number of younger couples anticipating marriage.

For people outside of DR Congo or other countries stereotyped as always being at war or always in famine, it can be difficult to imagine that life goes on in such troubled lands. It does. People suffer, yes, but they also live as normally as they can. Tragedies such as the murder of Pastor Nzelenga and his son are real and horrible. But we cannot, should not, lose sight of the fact that people still live, fall in love, wish to marry and have families. That they need the counsel of members such as Mwanza and Angélique, that the hope the church offers can be found in its dealing with larger issues and problems, and it can be found in the actions of its ordinary members.

Special thanks to Robert Neufeld, without whose help, passion and direction this chapter would not have been possible.

(opposite) *Meeting to chat after church at Shambumbu near Kajiji.*

(above) The Blessing *by Mukalay. A search for peace. A cry for God's guidance.*

surface area: 1,127,127 sq. km.
capital: Addis Ababa
population: 70.7 million (2003)
language: Amharic, Tigrinya, Orominga
major religion: Ethiopian Orthodox 35%-40%, Islam 40%-45%,
animist 15%-20%, other 5%
literacy: 28%
life expectancy: 45 (men), 46 (women)
annual income per capita: US $100

United Nations Human Development Index: 169 out of 175
countries (2003)

Mennonite World Conference Member Church

Name: Meserete Kristos Church
Local churches: 275
Members: 98,025

Gift Highlights: Choirs, writers, editors, evangelists, missionaries;
welcomes theological teacher/
student exchanges; "One Year
for Christ" evangelism program

Ethiopia

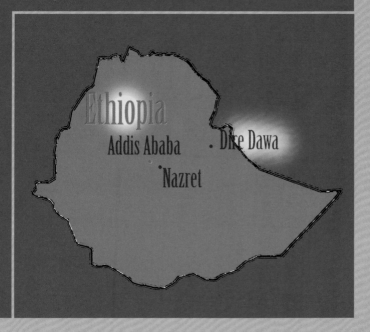

K enna Dula and Aster Wolde begin each day early. The cool predawn air of Ethiopia's highlands fills their home as they rise to pray together. Askale, their maid, awakens about the same time, around 5:00 a.m.

Kenna, Aster, their four children — Meheret (14), Amanuel (13), Peniel (10) and Shalom (8) — and Askale live in Akaki, a town just outside Ethiopia's large capital, Addis Ababa. Kenna works in the offices of the Meserete Kristos Church (MKC) in Addis. Meserete Kristos translates from the Amharic to "Christ is the Foundation." MKC is possibly the fastest growing of all the churches relating to Mennonite World Conference.

Kenna and Aster's family lives in a pleasant home in a newer area of Akaki, at the very edge of town. Within a minute's walk from their place Ethiopia's beautiful, timeless countryside opens, empty to the horizon — an endless expanse of unfenced farmland, broken by dry, rounded mountains. Akaki is known as a poor town on Addis' outskirts. At the edge of the city, it attracts country folk to its sprawling Saturday market which takes over seemingly every bit of the center of the town. Myriad vendors and buyers mingle, creating a festive atmosphere. Children play a kind of skipping game in dry ditches. People come not only to eke out a living and to buy goods but to visit and share the latest news and gossip. Most things are cheaper than at Addis' immense and incredible central market, Mercato. Mercato is one of Africa's great market experiences but is not for the naive or faint of heart. Akaki's market does not offer as much, but it definitely offers better prices for all but the most skilled bargainers.

Dozens of donkeys, Ethiopia's ever present beast of burden both in the country and in the city, are tied together along the margins of the market in several places. They stand in tight knots, waiting for their owners to finish their business. Then they are reloaded and led back to their respective villages and farms within short and distant walks of Akaki.

Materially, Ethiopia is undeniably one of the poorest countries on earth. There have been and will be famines here. The country has lapsed into many wars. All the negatives that abound about the country are true to a point, but to let those overwhelm the outside perception of the country or to believe they involve every citizen is utterly wrong. When God created the world he gifted Ethiopia with an extra measure of astounding natural beauty. Its

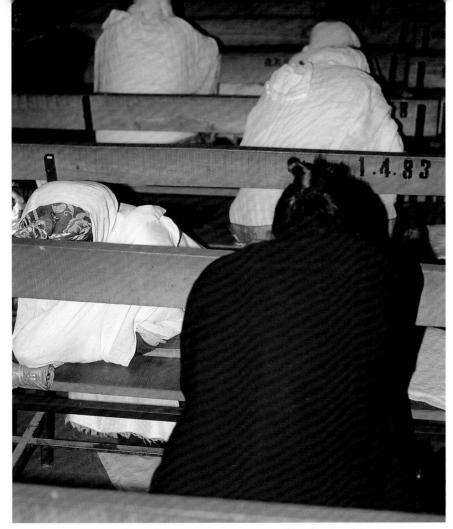

Women praying at a Friday night prayer service in Semen Addis church, Addis Ababa. (opposite) A children's Saturday program at the MKC church in Akaki.

highlands, deep gorges, lakes and mountains are spectacular. The country's wealth does not stop there. Its history is unlike any other in Africa. It had nearly 3,000 years of emperors, ending only in the 1970s when Haile Selassie was overthrown. It also has an ancient African church — the Ethiopian Orthodox Church founded at Axum in the 4th Century; a complex tribal history and a long penetration by Islam from the east. These and other features have created a unique country. Culturally and artistically Ethiopia is a rich and bountiful land.

After praying on their knees at their bedside, Kenna and Aster prepare for breakfast and work. Askale starts breakfast and begins to make coffee. Coffee is much more than a drink in Ethiopia. Its preparation is rich in tradition and an important and revered part of Ethiopian culture. Its cultural significance

has held strong through the centuries, through good times and bad.

The fact that Kenna and Aster employ a live-in maid does not mean they are wealthy. In Ethiopia maids are in many homes, from the wealthy ones to the quite poor. There is much to do and there are few modern conveniences even for those, like Kenna and Aster, who belong to Ethiopia's middle class. Aster and her eldest daughter Meheret are also actively involved in the housework, even though Askale works in the home from before sunrise to bedtime.

Once the children have been fed and have left for school, Aster and Kenna depart for their jobs. Aster works as an accountant at a nearby factory on the road towards Debre Zeit. She and Kenna leave together and walk to the highway a few blocks away. Aster crosses the road and waits for a bus. Kenna bids his wife good-bye and traverses a rocky field down a slight hill towards the main road running through the heart of Akaki. A few boys sit beside the path breaking rocks which they will sell for road beds and at construction sites.

Horse-drawn carts wheel up and down the bumpy dirt tracks alongside the field. Kenna passes a factory, its doors just opening and employees streaming in for the day's work. He reaches the bottom of the hill and Akaki's main street. Boys play table tennis on two tables set at awkward angles in the dirt under an electrical pylon. Kenna stops beside the road near the ping pong players. Horse carts, the cheapest means of transport, large buses and blue and white public transport vans rush by.

Women stream by on foot. Some wear their netella — the thin, white cotton shawl traditionally worn around the shoulders or head and shoulders by Ethiopian women — with the decorative trim at the bottom. Some turn their netella so the trim is at the top. This indicates they are in mourning.

Finally a van stops and brings Kenna to the center of Akaki. There he boards a bus and waits, sometimes for 20 or more minutes, as the bus fills. Vendors walk the narrow aisle until the ticket taker begins to haul out rough, handmade stools stored under several seats. These are placed in the aisle so more people can be seated. Once the driver and ticket taker have determined that the bus is full enough it departs for Addis.

Along the way, with the bus already filled to overflowing, it stops and picks up more passengers. Somehow an extra centimeter is found here and there, and more bodies meld together. Lastly, when it seems no more could possibly fit, the ticket taker, who has been outside the bus recruiting passengers and ushering them onto the bulging vehicle, somehow squeezes in and the door shuts.

Eventually the bus pulls into the transport terminus outside Addis' downtown stadium. Kenna dismounts and cuts across in front of the stadium.

Young men are already playing soccer in a nearby muddy field. At the next street Kenna hails a blue and white van. It heads into the massive Meskal Square, a vast expanse of pavement that can fill with hundreds of thousands for special Orthodox events. During the Dergue's* time it featured huge portraits of Marx and Engels on a surrounding wall. Streets connect to the square at both ends from several angles. Once in the square, driving becomes, to a visitor at least, a free-for-all. The square has no demarcated lanes. Vans, taxis, buses and cars burst out of their streets, squirting in every direction into the vast freedom of the square. Then it is a race to the other side, where they realign themselves and head out of the square to regular roads again.

Kenna reaches his final stop along the Bole Road and walks the last five minutes to the church offices. He passes shops, homes, restaurants, beggars, a computer training school, a few women selling fruit and vegetables spread before them. The MKC offices are around the corner and down a hill from the Bole Church.

Emperor Haile Selassie was overthrown by radical Marxists in 1974. This led to years of wretched rule by the dictator Mengistu Haile Mariam and the Dergue. In 1982 the Dergue expropriated the Bole Church and turned it into a school and a Marxist indoctrination center. MKC leaders were rounded up and thrown into prison. No charges were ever brought against them. They existed in appalling conditions. Cells were so crowded all the prisoners had to agree to move together or they were unable to turn. At irregular intervals, individuals, seemingly randomly, were removed and executed. Bodies were dumped on street corners. Relatives had to pay the government to recover corpses for proper burial. Whenever someone was taken out everyone in the cell believed it was to be executed. Four years after being arrested the MKC leaders were suddenly taken out. They expected the worst. Instead they were dumped alive at a street corner and left to find their way home.

At the time when the leaders were arrested the MKC church had approximately 5,000 members. Then the church went underground, and largely disappeared from the outside world. The Dergue was ousted in 1991. The church reemerged 34,000 strong. During the time of the worst imaginable persecution the church thrived. Its explosive growth continues to this day. In early 2003 the church reported approximately 100,000 baptized believers and about 200,000 people attending the 275 church congregations and almost 600 house churches throughout Ethiopia and even in Eritrea.

An hour and a half after leaving home, Kenna enters the MKC office he shares with Kassa Agafari. They begin their work day. The smell of roasting coffee beans from a kitchen in the back drifts through the window.

*The Dergue was a military committee led by the Marxist dictator Mengistu Haile Mariam. They ruled Ethiopia with a ruthless iron fist from 1974 to 1991, when they were overthrown.

(this page) A few of the normal responsibilities for Meheret Kenna; doing her sister Shalom's hair, washing clothes, roasting coffee beans.

(opposite) Amanuel Kenna sets off for school; Aster Wolde waits for transport to her job; Meheret helps her mother wash her hands before eating; Kenna Dula helps Shalom with her homework.

(clockwise from bottom left) Kenna Dula, Kassa Agafari and Girma Teklu in the cavernous Miserak Addis church, the largest MKC church with 2,500 members and 18 full-time staff. Dula, Agafari and Teklu work in the MKC conference offices — Dula in the pastoral department headed by Agafari while Teklu is the conference leader. The pastoral department prepares ordinances for the whole church. Agafari and Dula travel often to all the regions of the country counseling elders and pastors, attending regional council meetings and making sure doctrine is sound in a church where many local pastors have little formal training.

The Miserak Addis church in Addis Ababa.

A worker at the MKC office.

Art from Tibebe Terffa's cross series. Terffa is one of Ethiopia's best known contemporary painters. His work is strongly influenced by his roots and his faith but has been made truly his own through experimenting with styles and forms.

One of the stone churches at Lalibela. Ethiopia has a rich and ancient artistic tradition unlike anywhere else in Africa. Much of the art comes out of the Ethiopian Orthodox church, which was founded in the 4th Century. The 11 stone churches at Lalibela in remote Wollo province were chiseled out from a mountainside about 850 years ago. To Ethiopians they are known as the Eighth Wonder of the World.

surface area: 752,614 sq. km.
capital: Lusaka
population: 10.8 million (2003)
language: English (official), Bemba, Lozi, Nyanja, Tonga
major religion: Christianity, indigenous beliefs, Hinduism, Islam
literacy: 78.9%
life expectancy: 33 (men), 32 (women)
annual income per capita: US $320

United Nations Human Development Index: 163 out of 175 countries (2003)

Mennonite World Conference Member Church

Name: Brethren in Christ Church
Local churches: 150
Members: 15,374

Gift Highlights: Handcraft teachers, church farms

Zambia

family stories

family stories

"Daddy, Daddy!" Chileleko cried joyously from across the shallow valley on the outskirts of Choma. Her father, Abert Seemani, smiled and said, "Chileleko means blessing." The setting sun, shimmering through the dust-drenched sky, outlined Chileleko's silhouette in burnt orange as she scampered through a field to reach the path that would bring her to her returning father. Her mother, Patricia Seemani, followed not far behind. The reunion after a few days apart was warm and filled with happy chatter.

Abert had been in his parents' village, Nakeempa, about 40 kilometers from the paved highway which connects Choma to Victoria Falls and the Zimbabwean border. Choma is a major town along the highway, and it is home to the Zambian Brethren in Christ (BIC) conference office. Nakeempa has a small central area with a few tiny shops, a BIC school, a bar and a BIC church. The community consists primarily of subsistence farms scattered about the area. Most of the family compounds are connected by narrow paths, rather than by roads. A few dirt tracks reach into the area from the recently re-paved highway. It is not unusual to go for days without seeing or hearing a vehicle.

Abert's family lives about half an hour's walk from the church, through rolling savannah. The church is at the center of their lives. Abert's father, Daniel, and his mother, Sophia, are Christian pillars in the community. Daniel has been a deacon for over 30 years. Now 71, he hopes to curtail his church activities, but he still oversees six congregations, some of which are three hours away by bicycle. He walks to the others. He visits the sick, seeks out those who have left the church, leads evangelical services and teaches baptismal classes. Daniel loves his work. This is evident in his relaxed demeanor. He smiles easily and has a welcoming air about him. His presence suggests a wise and compassionate man, at ease in his surroundings and grounded in his faith.

The Seemani's compound is larger and busier than most. Tiny houses with thatched roofs, a cooking shack, a shelter for grinding corn, some small, rough granaries, shelters for animals and a tiny dried grass walled bathing enclosure dot the neatly swept yard. A fire pit beside the grinding shelter is the center of social life. Visitors come and go. Many neighbors come to use the Seemani's grinder because they don't have one.

Animals abound — pigs, cows, chickens, goats, dogs. The goats and cows leave each morning to wander free in the countryside. One afternoon, an hour's walk from the compound, we crossed paths with many goats. They belonged to the Seemanis. Unfailingly the goats and cows return later in the day to spend the night — the goats at dusk, and the cows shortly after dark. As the sun sets the chickens gather from all over the compound and line up under a low, wide tree near the fire pit. Supervised by a large rooster, one by one the hens flail their way up into the crown of the tree, argue vigorously over which will sit where and eventually settle in quietly for the night — plump, feathery bobbles in the branches.

The times are difficult. In 1997 the family had 45 cows. A disease outbreak took most of them. Now there are only three cows left. Drought will potentially lead to the Seemanis running out of dried corn, their staple food source, two months before the next harvest. But the cadence of life on the compound did not suggest heightened worry. Reliance on God to see them through was strongly felt.

Each night supper was shared in Daniel and Sophia's small two-room house. One night, while eating nsima, the corn based staple, and chicken, Abert quietly revealed his winding story of love lost and found. In dim, flickering candle light, Abert softly turned a conversation that had been about nothing much towards his life, his faith, and his family.

In 1995 Abert's first wife, Liliance, died suddenly after they had been married only five months. Abert had left a seemingly healthy partner to go to a youth camp. Liliance collapsed while pounding cornmeal. Abert returned home to find his wife had died. Her shocking death caused Abert to look closely at the fragility of life. He dreamt often of the need to bring people to Christ while there was still time.

God gave him the strength to avoid a traditional ritual cleansing to free his

Abert, Chileleko and Patricia Seemani. (opposite) Sunset at the BIC school in Choma.

home of his wife's spirit. This was a moment of personal triumph. The pressure was immense to make sure, according to custom, that his wife's spirit would leave the home and leave Abert at peace.

Traditional beliefs still cause the church concern said BIC conference overseer Reverend Leonard Hamasele. Rev. Hamasele accompanied Abert and I back to Choma from Nakeempa. On the way we stopped at Rev. Hamasele's mother-in-law's. Her husband had passed away three months earlier. Fearing her dead husband's spirit she still had trouble sleeping in her home. Rev. Hamasele felt she might decide to abandon her house, to admit defeat to ancient superstitions. After a few minutes of pleasantries everyone entered the home. Bible verses were read. All present then dropped to their knees on the dirt floor of the old woman's home. Tears flowed while prayers were quietly offered from around the kneeling circle. As we left Rev. Hamasele reassured his mother-in-law telling her that he would return soon and that God was with her.

Abert felt his dreams to bring people to Christ and his strength to resist the ritual cleansing were God directing him to the pastorate. He felt called to go to Bible College.

He did not feel like remarrying.

Liliance's death had left Abert disillusioned, thinking he would never find love, believing he could not bear to face the pain again of a loved one dying.

Far from Nakeempa, Patricia completed teacher training in Kitwe. She wanted to be stationed in Zambia's Copper Belt or in Lusaka, the capital. To her dismay she was sent to Nakeempa. She knew no one in the tiny community far from the more urban life she desired. Depressed she traveled south and, once past Choma, off the paved ribbon along dirt tracks into the endless savannah to Nakeempa.

Abert noticed the stranger in church. He greeted her regularly after church but did not get to know her beyond that. Then one Sunday he felt God prompting him to tell Patricia he loved her. He glanced at her during the service. How could he tell someone he barely knew that he loved her? He was unable to concentrate on the sermon. The thought that he must tell her of his love would not leave him. It blocked out all else. Immediately after church, while people mingled outside, Abert approached Patricia and professed his love. Coming out of the blue from a virtual stranger, Patricia was taken aback but flattered. She softly said, "Sorry, but I already have a boyfriend." Abert thanked her, wished her well and left for home.

Abert accepted that his telling Patricia he loved her had led to nothing. However, it had rekindled his desire to find a life's partner. He prayed that God would show him someone else. He looked about the church and saw no one who interested him. Nothing happened. In tiny Nakeempa the options of whom to meet were slim. He slipped back into resignation. His lot was to be single, he thought.

Abert went on with his life. Patricia continued to teach at Nakeempa's school. They saw each other each Sunday in church.

Some months later, during the church service, Patricia approached Abert and, just as out of the blue as Abert's earlier profession, whispered, so no one else would hear, "I agree to love you." His heart leapt. The rest of that morning's service was a blur.

As Abert relayed the story his eyes were filled with wonder and love. In a world where extreme material poverty is the norm he was a rich man — rich in the love of his wife, his daughter, his extended family and parents in Nakeempa, in the love of his Lord and Savior.

When Abert returned to Choma, where Patricia now teaches and they live, a man who once felt lost and alone was greeted by a loving child and wife. Chileleko is a blessing, a blessing come out of her father's recovery from doubt and sorrow and out of her mother's being assigned to a school and community she did not want to be a part of, a blessing enthusiastically reflecting the love evident in her small family, a pin prick of joy and hope deep in the beautiful, unending savannah of southern Africa.

Scenes from the Seemani compound in Nakeempa: (above) women gather to strip dried corn from their husks and to visit — Sophia Seemani sits highest in the photo; (left) Daniel Seemani's bicycle used to make his rounds as deacon for six congregations; (far left) kids at the family corral.

Two women prepare for church on Sunday morning.

(right) Abert Seemani, left, chats with the Nakeempa pastor after Sunday service.

(far right) Women and girls during congregational singing in Nakeempa's Brethren in Christ church.

(left) Children wrapped to protect themselves against the early morning dry season chill.

(above) Daniel and Sophia Seemani's compound shortly after daybreak.

(below) Daniel Seemani relaxes in his favorite chair near the fire pit that serves as the social gathering area.

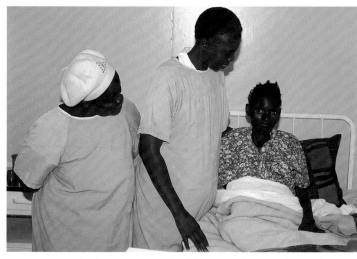

A nurse, Lastinah Shamapani — wife of former Brethren in Christ bishop Enock Shamapani, and an AIDS patient in a new hospice in Choma. HIV/ AIDS is a terrible plague in southern Africa. This hospice was set up to allow suffering people a decent, clean place where their lives can conclude surrounded by caring, loving staff in an atmosphere designed to give the patients as much peace and dignity as possible.

Preparing the next meal in the Seemani compound. A still fortunate chicken surveys the situation.

A neighbor of the Seemani's at the long shadowed end of another dry season day.

HAPPY WOMEN COMING FROM SHOPRITE CHECKERS IN MONGU.

(inset) Happy
Shoppers *by Stephen
Kappata, well known
for his light hearted
takes on Zambian
daily life.*

Shadows *by Pato
Kabwe reflects the
calm, rhythm and
beauty of a typical sun
drenched, shadow
dappled day.*

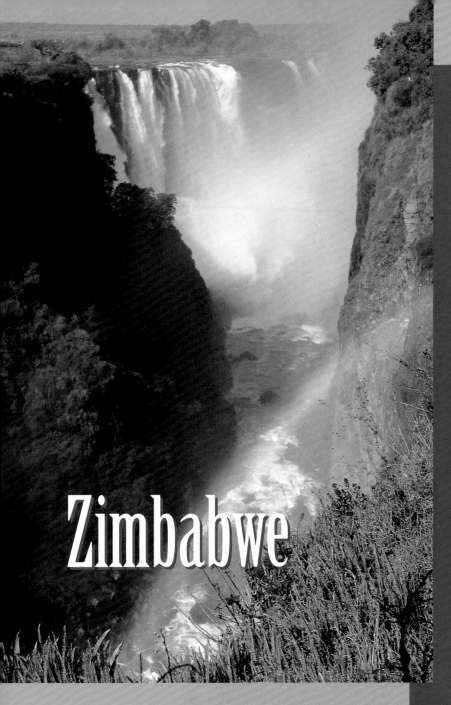

Zimbabwe

surface area: 390,580 sq. km.
capital: Harare
population: 12.9 million (2003)
language: English (official), Shona, Sindebele
major religion: Christianity, indigenous beliefs
literacy: 85%
life expectancy: 34 (men), 33 (women)
annual income per capita: US $480

United Nations Human Development Index:
145 out of 175 countries (2003)

Mennonite World Conference Member Church

Name: Ibandla Labazalwane ku Kristu e Zimbabwe
Local churches: 272
Members: 29,213

Gift Highlights: Church growth resources, experience with
women's programs

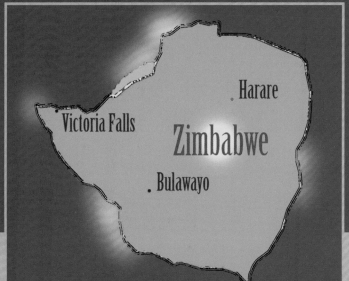

family stories

When westerners speak of poverty — the worst kind of poverty — they usually think of Africa. Materially, many African countries do have more than their share of extreme poverty, but labeling a place as hopeless simply because of a lack of material wealth creates an incomplete picture. Zimbabwe — despite huge obstacles — is a country with countless examples of people exuding the positive spirit and energy that is found in much of Africa and is obvious to any visitors who make the effort to meet the ordinary people. Unfortunately this spirit cannot be demonstrated statistically. It is not immediately obvious when looking in from the outside.

Ronald Lizwe Moyo and his wife Su exude such a positive spirit. They live at Emthunzini Wethemba House, a home for street children near the Mzilikazi area of Bulawayo, Zimbabwe's second largest city.

Bulawayo is a lovely, relaxed city. It is sprawled over dry, scrubby terrain not far from the Matopos, an area of extraordinary jumbled rock formations. Townships — leftovers from the days of white-ruled Rhodesia — ring the city, creating its sprawl. The downtown area retains a sleepy ambiance, quite different from most other large African cities. Wide avenues — carved out of the bush in order to give Cecil Rhodes' huge wagons enough room to turn round in

one swoop — give Bulawayo's downtown a distinctly different look from any other African city. A beautiful city park points visitors from the edge of downtown to one of Africa's most pleasant natural history museums.

The Brethren in Christ (BIC) conference maintains its offices in downtown Bulawayo. The building includes one of two downtown BIC bookstores. Su operates a small seamstress shop upstairs. Ronald works at Emthunzini.

A bland cement wall surrounds Emthunzini, hiding the activity inside. A C-shaped string of buildings curves around the back of the large courtyard. At the left end of the "C" is the director's house, and on the right side is Ronald and Su's home. They are the only staff. Up to 56 children reside at Emthunzini. Ronald and Su have two small children of their own, Lincoln and Linda. Linda is a precocious toddler who feels as though she is living with dozens of big brothers and sisters. She cruises the compound, playing and "helping" wherever she can. Besides looking after the street children and their two, Ronald and Su have taken in two orphaned sisters, Norma and Abigail, as their own. Life is full.

Ronald has a sun-filled office in their home. It overlooks the courtyard through an open door and a large window. As he works, his own kids and the resident street children, come and go. As a result of the lack of staff, the resident children are responsible for many of the duties in the home — cooking, baking, cleaning, washing, and even leading Bible studies. Ronald's calm, good natured, Christ-centered personality seems to flow through the place.

The residents range in age up to 18. Some of them are orphans, others are troubled kids whose families could not handle them, and some were abandoned for economic reasons. At least one is HIV positive. All the residents are supposed to go to school. They seem to thrive in this firm but loving atmosphere. Discipline generally is not a major problem. Ronald quietly fields many requests, concerns and complaints on a daily basis. Girls invariably sit on their knees, a traditional sign of respect, in the doorway as they bring their appeals to Ronald. His wise and compassionate responses help the place keep an even keel.

Several afternoons each week some of the resident boys pull out a collection of marimbas and begin to play. The smaller boys and the girls begin to dance. Lincoln and Linda join the party. In these children, under the loving guidance of Ronald, hope can be seen in a country which some portray as hopeless. The African spirit, mysterious to the outsider, rolls on.

The church is central in Ronald and Su's life. Ronald loves to sing and he participates in as many choirs as possible, at both the congregational and national conference levels. Each Sunday they leave their compound and walk up the road in the direction of downtown. They stop where another road intersects

Sukoluhle (Su) and Ronald Lizwe Moyo in church.

(opposite) Spectacular Victoria Falls.

Pleasant downtown Bulawayo (above) and daily activity in one of the city's townships.

with theirs and they wait for transport to arrive. Eventually a van comes to a stop in front of them. They ask where it is headed. If it's going in their direction, they squeeze in with the other passengers, and they're on their way. Once downtown, they disembark and make their way up a crowded street, full of market stalls, to a pick-up point. Here they wait for another van. After an hour or so they arrive at their township church, Pumula.

One Sunday when I accompanied Ronald and Su to church we stopped at relatives on the way home. There was much activity in front of the neat, small house. One of the daughters was going to get married soon. The groomsmen and bridesmaids were practicing for the reception. It is the attendants' responsibility to put together some choreographed dancing for the reception. The mood was light but still serious because the choreographed numbers are an important part of the wedding day.

Ronald and I went for a walk in the township. As we meandered along I began to notice young people dancing in front of several homes, all practicing for weddings.

Eventually we found another van and made our way homeward. Ronald suggested we get out about half an hour's walk from our destination. As colors warmed and dust dulled the sky in the late winter afternoon, we passed through some fields. We saw people working in vegetable patches and boys playing soccer with twine balls on a pitch of grass scorched gold and baked earth.

We made our way to a large hospital to visit one of Ronald's sick relatives. He wanted me to see the Zimbabwe that is filled with the intangible African spirit. He also wanted me to see some other realities, not to shock me or to make me feel sorry but simply to say these things are real, too, just like the positive energy and stalwart spirits of people like Ronald and Su are real. To negatively stereotype a people out of ignorance is wrong, and it is also wrong to go too far in the other direction by over-romanticizing them.

The hospital was clean. Wide halls led to large, airy wards. We walked past rows of beds. Some patients looked okay. Others, obviously already beyond their last feeble struggle against HIV/AIDS, simply waited for death. It was Sunday afternoon. Many families were visiting. Pockets of the room, where relatives sat beside listless loved ones or where lonely patients, gaunt and nearly gone, had come to merely existing were quiet. But the overall atmosphere sounded almost festive as friends and family chatted.

Ronald introduced me to his cousin. She was in and out of hospital on a regular basis. This time she was there because of a nose bleed that wouldn't stop. Her immune system was slowly crashing. She appeared tired and tentative but looked forward to going home the next day.

She sat up. "What's it like overseas? Where are you from?" she asked.

"Canada," I replied.

"Everybody wants to go to Canada or the UK. Are there jobs?" She said this with some sad hope in her voice.

Ronald and I stayed at her side awhile longer, then said goodbye and were on our way.

Su, Norma and Abigail were busy preparing supper when we arrived home. Lincoln and Linda were playing a version of soccer in the long narrow hallway. Linda was ecstatic each time she kicked the ball. Her smile, mischievous twinkle and whoops of uncontrollable joy were enough to melt the heart of the hardest person.

Ronald's parents had come to the city from their village. They would stay with Ronald and Su for as long as they wished.

There was a knock on the door. A family of relatives — mother, father and several children — arrived unannounced. Su, Norma and Abigail, with seeming joy, quickly began to figure out how to extend the food to fill the stomachs of unanticipated guests. The hallway soccer game turned into a raucous dance as more children joined the chaotic fray. Happy, boisterous conversation filled the home. I asked Ronald what they thought of the arrival of so many guests right at the supper hour. He beamed, "It is normal. They are family." He shrugged nonchalantly.

Outside, life went on. Negative statistics continued to pile up, but inside countless other homes in Zimbabwe decent, godly people were leading lives — beyond statistics, beyond the news — that offered reason for hope: hope for a beautiful country created by God's loving hands; hope coming through people filled with a positive, generous spirit, readily evident even in times of great turmoil — a hope that they attribute to their Lord and Savior.

Linda Moyo and her grandfather, Rodger Moyo.

Life at Emthunzini; kids cleaning and knitting, Ronald at work.

(clockwise from far left) Preparing for a wedding reception dance. Su dishing out the evening meal. Mothers in Sunday school. Ronald and Su waiting for transport to take them to church.

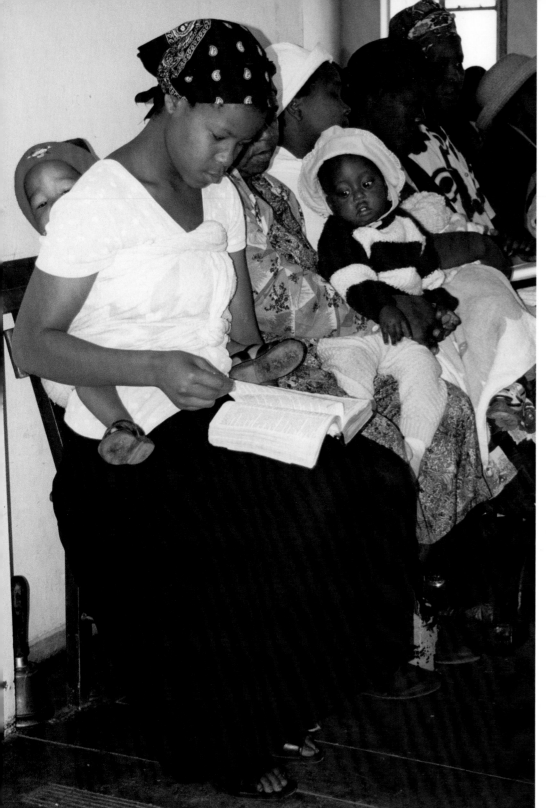

(clockwise from far left) Bible reading during church. A small child waiting outside a church. Teenage girls after church.

Ngotha Imbawula, *acrylic on paper by Bulawayo artist Tomy Ndebele. (inset) Detail from another acrylic painting by Tomy Ndebele.*

surface area: 110,860 sq. km.
capital: Havana
population: 11.3 million (2003)
language: Spanish
major religion: Catholic, Protestant, Santería
literacy: 94%
life expectancy: 75 (men), 79 (women)
annual income per capita: n/a

United Nations Human Development Index: 52 out of 175 countries (2003)

Mennonite World Conference Member Church

Name: Sociedad Misionera Hermanos en Cristo
Local churches: 80
Members: 2,000

Gift Highlights: Puppets, sugar technology, computer training

Cuba

La Habana (Havana)

Cuba

Santiago de Cuba

family stories stories

Cuba. For Canadians and Europeans Cuba is a land of beaches, warm sun, all-inclusive resorts, Old Havana. Many visit it every year to escape winter's chill. For many it is also a place of some curiosity and admiration due to the fact this small, poor nation has thumbed its nose at its giant, wealthy neighbor for decades. This does not mean there is agreement with the politics of the island but most often rather simply respect for its determination to say no to a nation so much bigger and more powerful than itself, one that expects to get its way. For most Americans Cuba is shrouded in mystery; it is forbidden fruit according to their government. During the prolonged Elián González saga some Cubans in Florida spread stories of a country where children were not loved, where the family unit had been destroyed.

Much can be debated with regards to politics. Both sides are right and wrong — Cubans, without a doubt, are not free; the country is run by a dictator; people are treated as if they cannot be trusted; but it also boasts far better health care than most materially poor countries; its life expectancy is literally decades longer than in some comparably poor countries and it rivals that of much richer countries. Cuba also has possibly the best education system of any impoverished country. Children are loved and cherished. While their freedoms erode as they get older, for the young Cuba is a wonderful, safe place.

Politics, both American and Cuban, confuse the picture of Cuba. Little is as clearly black and white as both sides insist. The true Cuba resides beyond tourism and politics. It can be found in a people who are warm and hospitable, in towns, cities and villages seemingly light years from the tourist beaches and the plaza designed for orchestrated protest across from the US Interest Section building on Havana's world famous Malecon.

The welcoming, giving nature of the people is beyond debate. Anyone fortunate enough to spend time with a Cuban family and community away from the tourist areas will be exposed to a culture that is attractive, incredibly sensual and comfortable, one that is a pleasure and an honor to experience — one that is difficult to leave.

Cuatro Caminos is a town of 4,000 about an hour's drive from

(opposite) A granddaughter and daughter of Jésus Lescano Peres and Maria E. Aguirre Calderon pose on their way home from school in Cuatro Caminos.

A woman from Nazareno who held onto her faith through the most difficult years. Now, for over a decade Cubans have openly lived and worshiped as Christians.

Pastor José Ernesto Martin Torres looking over Nazareno. He yearns for more teaching on what it is to be an Anabaptist Christian.

Havana. The Roca Eterna Brethren in Christ (BIC) church is on the main street. The thriving, spirited church led by Bishop Daniel Cabrera Coca and his wife Sarah Pérez de Cabrera was the first BIC church in Cuba. Maria Regla Reyes Coto, a single mother of a teenage son, is a member of Roca Eterna. Maria is vice-treasurer for the BIC in Cuba. Maria's front door opens at the break of dawn, as is common. It stays open until the last person goes to bed. If the door is open, people can enter unannounced. And they do. Throughout the day friends, relatives and passers-by walk through the open door to visit, to say hello, to borrow something they do not have, and to lend something Maria does not have. Children play in the street. On their way home from school they veer into the house to give a quick kiss and be on their way. Community spirit, the sense of people looking out for each other is strong.

On Valentine's Day a party began across the street from Maria's in the late afternoon. Cuban beer and rum flowed freely. The early start to the partying caused it to fizzle to a muddled, quiet stop before midnight. The party-goers had run out of energy and liquor. Maria was watching television. Her door was still open. A drunken, middle-aged woman staggered into view on the sidewalk across the street. She struggled to stay on her feet. In the darkness the silhouette lurched along as if the sidewalk was a narrow ribbon of rope. She clutched at a chain link fence for balance. Her progress was pitifully slow. Maria noticed the woman, immediately got up and quietly walked across the street. She grasped the woman by the arm and guided her gently down the street. Fifteen minutes later Maria returned having taken the woman to her home several blocks away. The drunken woman was not her friend, nor a relative. Yet, Maria, without hesitation, went to her aid. She was reacting as both a Christian and a Cuban.

José Ernesto Martin Torres was engaged to be married in 1999. He was 25 and on course to become a BIC pastor. The bishop saw leadership potential in the young man. Ernesto felt his path was set — a family and a life of service within the church as God wished.

Then his fiancée went to the US to visit relatives. She did not return. Several months later Ernesto received a devastating letter. His fiancée had found someone else. She no longer loved him. Ernesto did not know what to do. He still loved her. He decided he had to leave Cuba, not for political or economic reasons, but for love. He wanted to win back the woman with whom he believed he was destined to spend his life.

The secretive process of leaving was set in motion. He felt he could tell no one of his plans. He found another young man willing to chance leaving. They headed to the coast and bought a small rowboat, complete with oars but no motor. They pushed off for Florida, somewhere beyond the horizon. They rowed unseen past the coast guard. They rowed four miles from shore. The ocean swells began to increase in size; what they had felt was a more than adequate boat began to feel very small. As Cuba faded and they faced a landless vista, Ernesto felt God talking to him. He stopped rowing and prayed. He was being called back to Cuba, to a country where his service as a pastor was needed.

Ernesto suggested to his companion that he wanted to return. The young man surveyed the now menacing sea and admitted the folly of two men in a row boat without a motor on the open ocean. He said he was scared and ready to go back, too. They swiveled the boat southward towards Cuba, rowed back undetected past the coast guard and made shore.

Upon his return the bishop suggested Ernesto become pastor of the El Pan de Vida church in Nazareno. Two months later Ernesto met a young woman. She loved the church. Sometime later she also came to love Ernesto.

Ernesto is engaged again. Happy and leading a small congregation that appreciates and loves their pastor, Ernesto said, smiling, "I met another woman. We fell in love. She is even more beautiful than the first."

Pastors Jésus Lescano Peres and Maria E. Aguirre Calderon lead the church, Rios de Agua Viva, in the tiny, impoverished pueblo of El Roble. El Roble is a miniscule, rural community, less than a blip on a map. As in many BIC churches, the pastorate in El Roble is definitely a team effort shared between husband and wife. Jésus and Maria are kind, gentle and on fire for Jesus Christ. Their loving relationship is a wonderful example to all around them. As they visit with friends or strangers, they instinctively touch each other, resting a loving hand on the other's shoulder, gently touching each other's arms as they chat. One cannot help but be comfortable in their presence. Their congregation, as in all BIC churches, gets together several times a week for services.

Wednesday morning is a prayer service. The Wednesday I visited, two women and an older man in a tattered military shirt attended. Even with the small turnout Jésus and Maria carried on with the service. They sang, read from the Bible and prayed. They prayed with great fervency. The older gentleman in the military shirt was obviously very poor. He was not a person most would regard as important. He was simply a poor campesino. But here, in the tiny church at El Roble, he was accepted and honored as equal, lovingly cherished and created in the image of God.

As I left Cuatro Caminos, Maria Regla Reyes Coto began to cry. Rivers of tears streamed down her dark cheeks. Language barriers did not prevent me from clearly seeing in her eyes that I was accepted and loved in her home and church.

When thinking about Cuba do not think of American or Cuban propaganda. Think of Jésus Lescano Peres and Maria E. Aguirre Calderon, think of José Ernesto Martin Torres, think of Maria Regla Reyes Coto. Think of our brothers and sisters passionately following Christ, helping the church to grow by leaps and bounds in tiny congregations in the biggest cities as well as in the smallest pueblos. Pray for them. Rejoice with them as they work to increase God's kingdom in a country made exceedingly beautiful by its common people.

Children outside the home of Jésus Lescano Peres and Maria E. Aguirre Calderon in Cuatro Caminos.

(this page, clockwise from top left) Jésus Lescano Peres and Maria E. Aguirre Calderon wait for transport in Cuatro Caminos to take them to their small church at El Roble.

Pastor Marcelino Mestre Elia with one of his parishioners from La Nueva Jerusalem church in the pueblo La Pesa.

Pastor Jésus Lescano Peres praying at a Wednesday morning prayer service in El Roble.

(opposite) The Roca Eterna church in Cuatro Caminos and worshippers.

BIC leader Felix Rafael Curbelo and Leyda Verde live in Rancho Boyeros, near Havana's airport. Their gracious hospitality and kindness to strangers is not atypical in Cuba.

(clockwise from top left) Rafael buying fresh coconut from the local private market.

Leyda visiting with a friend in front of her home.

Pork for sale in the Rancho Boyeros private market. Pork is the most common meat eaten in Cuba.

Painting by Bauta based artist Cheleni.
Art by chance in Nazareno.

Curitiba photo collage by Aldo Rempel

Brazil

surface area: 8,511,965 sq. km.
capital: Brasília
population: 178.4 million (2003)
language: Portuguese
major religion: Catholic 68%, Protestant 10.43%, spiritism

literacy: 83.3%
life expectancy: 64 (men), 73 (women)
annual income per capita: US $3,070

United Nations Human Development Index: 65 out of 175 countries (2003)

Mennonite World Conference Member Churches

Name: Associação das Igrejas Menonitas do Brasil
Local churches: 6
Members: 772

Name: Associação Evangélica Menonita
Local churches: 30
Members: 2,000

Gift Highlights: International dialogue, sports clubs, cross cultural mission workers, marriage counselors

family stories

As friends and relatives died around them or were disappearing into the black hole of Stalin's gulag, David Klassen's family decided to flee from their long-established home in Russia. Klassen, like many other German-speaking boys and young men fleeing Russia, was forced into the German army when he fled. As the Germans retreated from Russia, Klassen was captured by the Russians and put into a prison camp. His family continued on and eventually escaped to Brazil.

Branded a traitor, Klassen was placed on death row. He saw many fellow prisoners taken out to be executed. He expected the worst but was spared. He readily thanks God for his deliverance when others around him in the camp were killed. After six years, following Stalin's death, he was finally released and then worked in Siberia and Tajikistan, where he also illegally served as a pastor. After retirement he was allowed to leave the Soviet Union and go to find his family in Curitiba, Brazil. He arrived in 1967.

When Mennonites first settled in the Curitiba area of Brazil's southern Parana State, beginning in 1935, they established farms 12 kilometers outside the city. Today those areas are long since swallowed by the city of two million.

The Mennonite community is still strong in Curitiba, and it now includes Brazilians other than the descendants of the first German-speaking settlers. A city park dedicated to the Mennonites, several churches and a school, Colégio Erasto Gaertner, with about 1,000 students, stamp the area the Mennonites first inhabited, Boqueirão. The majority of the school's students are no longer from Mennonite families. They attend the school because of its good reputation. A smaller Mennonite Brethren school is nearby. Students at both schools wear track suits as school uniforms.

There is also a Mennonite-operated personal care home in Curitiba. Not all the residents are Mennonites. The home, like Colégio Erasto Gaertner, indicates that the original German-speaking Mennonites have to a large degree integrated into Brazilian society. While not abandoning the German language, Portuguese is now the first language of many.

The personal care home is full of myriad stories, some sad, some inspirational. A trip down the halls leads past long-lived journeys behind each door.

Annie Wieler Dyck at 82, frail and confined to a wheelchair, shares her room with and still takes care of her middle-aged mentally handicapped daughter. Resident Liese Giesbrecht has recently had a stroke. Paralyzed, she no longer is able to care for herself. Fellow resident Agatha Unruh stands alongside Giesbrecht's wheelchair, lovingly brushing and braiding her long gray hair — each tender stroke of the brush is a moment of gentle therapy from a friend. A family photo in the room from years past shows a large,

happy, healthy family. Giesbrecht stands young, confident and beautiful in the front row surrounded by parents and siblings. All are now deceased. Alone, Giesbrecht relies on the help of the home's staff and the love shown in the kindness of friends like Unruh.

David Klassen is also a resident at the personal care home. At 94 he still leads Bible studies each morning for some residents. Overwhelmingly Klassen is known as a thankful and kind man. Even after having gone through much hardship, not finding a place of peace until retirement age and learning upon arriving in Brazil that his wife, believing her husband had been killed, was remarried, Klassen did not lose his generous, gentle spirit. Peter Siemens, a local Mennonite leader, says admiringly that even though Klassen has gone through so much he remains a positive and inspiring person.

It is difficult to imagine a more positive person than Peter Pauls. He and his wife Anne live in Witmarsum colony about an hours' drive from Curitiba through the green, gently rolling countryside. The center of Witmarsum is in the hollow of a bowl in the terrain. Lush green pastures spread up and out of the hollow from the small village at the bottom. The road reaching into the heart of the community of approximately 1,200 Mennonites and 1,000 others who toil in the colony passes the Pauls' home before reaching the bottom. An informative museum stands alongside a reservoir near the colony school in the village center. The colony cooperative and drab industrial complex are across a dusty

Peter and Anne Pauls

parking lot. Heading up the hill on the opposite side the road passes two Mennonite churches, General Conference and Mennonite Brethren, within a short walk of each other.

Many of Witmarsum's non-Mennonite workers come from Brazil's poverty stricken northeast. Mennonites from Witmarsum have done some mission work there. Through these contacts some families were brought to Witmarsum to work. Others followed, hearing of the better economic opportunities in the south.

The Pauls' home cannot be missed coming into the colony. A wide, immaculate yard fronts the road. An endless formation of flowers, thick blasts of vivid color, line the road's edge

blasts of vivid color, line the road's edge the entire length of the property. The house, up a hill, is surrounded by flowers — in flower beds, in window boxes, wherever Anne can plant them. At the crest of the driveway a small dog pretends to be brave and fearless but retreats quickly into the safety of his dog house the instant a stranger turns his way. A barn is behind the house as the hill begins to slope down, opening a lovely country view of layer after layer of green to the horizon.

The Paulses are a hospitable couple open to family and visitors alike. They take on their role as grandparents with relish. It's very obvious that their grandchildren enjoy staying for the night. When grandchildren are staying over, they are Peter and Anne's first priority. Peter spends much of the evening reading with them and telling stories — books read and stories told not out of a feeling of a grandfather's obligation but with joy. "An Opa must read to his grandchildren," he says with a broad grin. Peter's exuberance is contagious as the children anticipate his every word.

Peter works for Menonita Beneficente (Mennonite Aid Association). His personality is well suited to the work of bringing aid and Christ to the poor of Parana state. Witmarsum looks idyllic. The highway through the countryside nearby is as good as any in much richer countries. Visiting Witmarsum and driving on the lovely highway it is difficult to imagine there is grinding poverty within reach. But there is.

Peter drives hours away from the main highway to reach forgotten communities where people scratch out meager existences. Menonita Beneficente reaches 270 poor communities in the state of Parana. The association does service and evangelism work, builds homes and gives out meals among other things. At Christmas they travel to various centers offering seasonal concerts.

Arnhold and Adriane Thiessen straddle the worlds of the original German-speaking Mennonites and that of the new Portuguese-speaking Mennonites. The Thiessens are both engineers, originally from Witmarsum, who now live and work in Curitiba. Ezequiel Alves is a fellow engineer and good friend from a Portuguese Mennonite congregation. In Parana, Paraguay's Chaco, in certain areas of Canada and the US Mennonites have been more defined by their ethnicity than anything else. That is changing in every case — sometimes more slowly, sometimes much more rapidly. Ezequiel, as other Portuguese Brazilians identifying themselves as Mennonites in churches from Sao Paulo to Brasilia, is breaking that old stereotype. His enthusiasm for the church is fresh and contagious. He, too, can claim the stories of his church as his own, such as those of heroes of the faith and family like David Klassen.

(this page) Peter Pauls with two of his grandchildren and the home of Peter and Anne Pauls in Witmarsum. (opposite) Flowers line the path to the Witmarsum Museum.

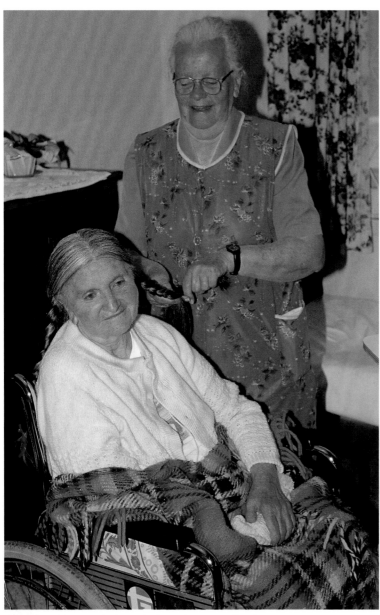

(above) Agatha Unruh doing the hair of Liese Giesbrecht.

(right) David Klassen at 94.

(left) Students of Colégio Erasto Gaertner in Curitiba.

(above) Henrique Ens in front of his family's crypt. The cemetery is located in what was once a Mennonite farmer's field in what is now the Boqueirão area of Curitiba.

(right) The Mennonite Brethren church in Boqueirão, Curitiba.

(right) Entering Witmarsum colony.

(below) Cornfields on the farm of Rosvita and Hardy Harder at Witmarsum. The Harders also operate a farm 2,000 kilometers to the north in Bahia state, where land is more plentiful and cheap.

Photo collage of old Curitiba by Aldo Rempel

Paraguay

surface area: 406,750 sq. km.
capital: Asunción
population: 5.9 million (2003)
language: Spanish, Guarani
major religion: Catholic 90%
literacy: 92.1%
life expectancy: 69 (men), 73 (women)
annual income per capita: US $1,350

United Nations Human Development Index: 84 out of 175 countries (2003)

Mennonite World Conference Member Churches

Name: Convención de las Iglesias Evangélicas Unidas
Local churches: 14
Members: 4,032

Name: Convención Evangélica de Iglesias Paraguayas de los Hermanos Menonitas
Local churches: 69
Members: 3,052

Name: Convención Evangélica Mennonita Lengua
Local churches: 7
Members: 2,084

Name: Convención Evangélica Menonita Paraguaya
Local churches: 27
Members: 1,203

Name: Convención Iglesias Evangélicas Hermanos Menonitas Nivaclé
Local churches: 8
Members: 2,260

Name: Evangelische Mennonitische Bruderschaft
Members: 55

Name: Vereinigung der Mennoniten Brüdergemeinden Paraguays
Local churches: 7
Members: 1,623

Name: Vereinigung der Mennonitengemeinden von Paraguay
Local churches: 19
Members: 7,231

Gift Highlights: Voluntary service program, mental health work, cross-cultural mission experience

(this page) Cattle, an important part of the Mennonite economy in the Chaco.

(opposite) Melvin and Gudrun Warkentin's children cause an explosion of butterflies in a ditch near Yalve Sanga.

Filadelfia

Paraguay

Asunción

family stories
stories

The hot Chaco sun scorched the baked earth around Margarete Bräul's empty Filadelfia home as she slowly shuffled towards the back door. The typically wide porch around the house shielded windows from the withering heat. Thick, dark curtains made sure the rooms inside would be as cool as possible. She stopped to look at some plants, wondering if they were being properly cared for. She fumbled in her bag for the keys and opened the door.

Bräul, now in her 80s, was the first Mennonite art teacher in the Chaco, an arid, mostly featureless area occupying a large chunk of Paraguay. She, like thousands of other German-speaking Mennonites fleeing persecution and death in Russia decades earlier, ended up in the Chaco. The Paraguayan government had said that if the Mennonites could subdue this land which no Europeans had been able to vanquish until then they would be welcome to make their new home there. The Mennonites joined the hunter/gatherer tribes indigenous to the area as the inhabitants of the Chaco. Three colonies were initially established — Fernheim, with Filadelfia as its principal community; Menno, started by Mennonites who left Canada, with Loma Plata at its core; and Neuland, with Neu Halbstadt as its main settlement. A fourth colony, Volendam, was established across the Paraguay River in east Paraguay, in the more densely populated region of the country where the land and weather are more hospitable.

In the Mennonite colonies' early years in the Chaco, life was extremely difficult. Some died of malnutrition. Eventually, through hard work, persistence, faith and ingenuity, they did subdue the land and the colonies became perhaps the most successful communities in the country. Their isolation, hundreds of kilometers from the capital, Asuncion, across a dust-drenched and forbidding landscape, along with their distinct culture and faith brought from Russia and their wealth compared to other parts of the country help to create the feeling that when entering the colonies one is entering separate countries within a country.

The colonies have their own insurance and health care systems. Margarete Bräul, after more than 40 years of teaching, had condensed her life to one room in the personal care home in Filadelfia, taking advantage of the programs in place for aging German Mennonites. When she was a young adult, she had wanted to study art in Russia but feared she'd be made to create propaganda for the Communist government, so she studied mathematics and chemistry instead. Art, however, remained her love, and once in Paraguay she quickly converted to being an art teacher.

Bräul wanted me to visit her house, only recently vacated for the move to the personal care home, so I could see some of her artwork. Leaving her art behind gave her faint hope she would return to her house someday. Her mind was still clear, but her legs barely responded. She opened her back door, flicked on the kitchen light, slowly passed the empty, turned-off and open refrigerator, stopped to straighten some things on a tiny table, noted some dust she would have to take care of and inched into her living room. She navigated a harrowing minefield of loose, cattle-hide throw rugs, each one capable of shifting and sending her crashing to the floor. She tenaciously and defiantly kept shuffling in minuscule skidding steps towards her bedroom and a trunk filled with her art and memories. She preferred not to push the stabilizing bars on her collapsible walker into their locked position. The walker, as a result, wheezed in and out like an accordion as she negotiated her way through the house, making it seem like an even more perilous journey.

We finally reached her art. One wood burning of the Chaco countryside was rather well done.

We turned and headed out of the house, turning off each light behind us. We passed the open, empty refrigerator. Bräul paused for a last look, turned off the final light. The house fell into silence and darkness.

No one spoke as we drove back to the personal care home. After helping her back to her room, Bräul asked that I take the wood burning to the Mennonite World Conference assembly in Zimbabwe. She said she could not make it there but hoped someday to see the artwork again, maybe in Winnipeg after her legs got better.

In Bräul's world, reflecting her own determined personality and community, art is ordered and structured, done correctly, following rules.

Argüello Raúl is an Enlhet — better known as the Lengua to the European settlers — Indian artist. He, too, is a Mennonite, one of many converts over the years among the local indigenous population. His art, like Bräul's, reflects his community. Whereas the Russian Mennonites arrived to subdue the Chaco, the indigenous peoples lived there for centuries, learning to live as a part of nature, taking what the land offered them, surviving — where others could not — by knowing the land.

In Bräul's wood burning of the Chaco countryside a fence runs through the middle of the scene — the land subdued as the ideal vision of the Chaco. In a drawing of the Chaco countryside by Raúl there is no sign of humanity's intrusion, only nature, plants, animals and birds without boundaries. His traditional ideal is the land free, with people existing as it allows.

Neither view of the Chaco is necessarily right nor wrong, just different. Throughout the global Anabaptist community there are many differences, but one important similarity exists, that all, regardless of background, are equal in the eyes of God. Each member created in His image. This truth can be seen and should be heralded in the Chaco where very different communities live in close proximity to one another.

Ernesto and Elsa Unruh live in the Enlhet settlement of Yalve Sanga. Some of the Enlhet have taken on ethnic Mennonite names, others have Spanish names, or a combination. Traditionally the Enlhet did not have names. They would relate a person to when and where they were born or what happened at that time.

The typical Yalve Sanga home is tiny, set well back from the road, and surrounded by large gardens. There are small, straight dirt roads, but people seem to walk the meandering paths between homes more than along the roads. Elsa's parents live in a small mud house in the Unruh's compound. A son and daughter-in-law and their two small children live next door. There are many dogs roaming free, as well as chickens and cats. A short walk into the grassland behind the house leads to a pen filled with goats. The vast Chaco stretches out silently in all directions.

At first glance the Chaco appears boring and unchanging. A closer look reveals an intriguing land, filled with bird, animal and insect life. It hosts an astonishing variety of plants and trees. The unusual bottle tree is a beautiful symbol of the region.

The day ends in Yalve Sanga with guiso, the traditional Enlhet stew. It is made in a pot of boiling water sitting on an open fire. The meal is followed by

The work of Christlicher Dienst, at Capiata and at a daycare in Asunción.

passing maté, a South American tea, around the circle of people ringing the fire. Each person drinks from the same metal straw, dug deep into a mixture that looks like a mass of twigs and leaves to the uninitiated. Water, hot or cold, depending on preference, is poured over the mixture. Conversation is as soft as the dying light of another day. The small fire dwindles to nothing and everyone goes to bed.

Drinking maté is common across a broad slice of South America. The immigrant Mennonites and the Indian Mennonites share a love of the tea. They also share a love of the land, one that came naturally to the Enlhet and one that came after years of hard labor to the German Mennonites.

German-speaking Mennonites also settled in the capital city, Asunción. Christlicher Dienst, a Paraguayan Mennonite voluntary service organization is based there. Its work includes running a home for street children, volunteers working at Capiata — an old folks home for the poor in San Francisco d'Assis, and operating a daycare in Asuncion. They also do extensive work with the mentally handicapped. Christlicher Dienst began in 1951 as a thank-you to Paraguay for allowing Mennonite young men to be exempt from military service. The Mennonites wanted to help the country in return. They began by opening a leprosy hospital, and in 1957 a mental hospital. Both have since been taken over by the government but still include heavy Mennonite involvement.

The Mennonites also run a large guesthouse in Asunción. People catch buses to the Chaco colonies in front of a small, decrepit restaurant a few doors down the street. The local Paraguayan owner is full of jokes and smiles, warming up the bleak little establishment.

After a long day the bus from Asunción arrives at its final destination, Filadelfia, at the heart of the colonies. The passengers disembark. They are a mixture of German Mennonites, Indians and other Paraguayans who have moved to the area to be a part of a better economy than exists generally in the country. Very different communities — there by being able to live within nature, there by being able to subdue the land and there to follow economic opportunity — exist side by side.

Filadelfia residents Margarete Bräul and Argüello Raúl see and appreciate different things in culture and in the land where they both live. But both belong equally to God's global Anabaptist family.

(left) Timoteo, one of the first Enlhet Christians. (above) Larita, daughter-in-law of
Ernesto and Elsa Unruh, begins to prepare guiso.

(opposite) The Belen church at Yalve Sanga; Enlhet children.
The General Conference Mennonite Church at Neu Halbstadt. David and Tina Goetz
get set for an evening motor scooter ride in Filadelfia.

Sharing maté, something common in the general, German Mennonite and Indian communities of Paraguay.

(above) Tina Neufeld and Lisa Timoteo doing handi-work common to each of their communities.

A wood burning of a Chaco scene by Margarete Bräul.

surface area: 176,220 sq. km.
capital: Montevideo
population: 3.4 million (2003)
language: Spanish
major religion: Catholic 66%, Protestant 2%, Jewish 2%
literacy: 97.3%
life expectancy: 72 (men), 79 (women)
annual income per capita: US $5,710

United Nations Human Development Index: 40 out of 175 countries (2003)

Mennonite World Conference Member Churches

Name: Consejo de las Congregaciones de los Hermanos Menonitas
Local churches: 9
Members: 258

Name: Convención de Iglesias Evangélicas Menonitas en Uruguay
Local churches: 9
Members: 455

Name: Konferenz der Mennonitengemeinden in Uruguay
Local churches: 4
Members: 507

Gift Highlights: Music, organization, children's ministries, missions, counseling, Biblical and theological teachers.

Uruguay

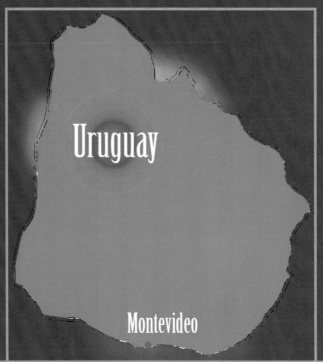

Uruguay

Montevideo

(above left) Old Montevideo. (opposite) A flea market in front of the cathedral in Old Montevideo — recent economic reality as opposed to just for fun.

A quick hop across the Rio de la Plata from Buenos Aires ends in Montevideo, Uruguay's gracious, faded capital. Montevideo is a some-what melancholy city in a country struggling through economic hard times which are largely the result of its dependence on its two much larger neighbors, Brazil and Argentina. When these countries hurt, so does Uruguay, but this is outside the purview of much of the world.

Horse-drawn carts are not uncommon in Montevideo, one of the most European-like cities in South America. Times are tough, but this does not mean that it is not an attractive city. It is one of the loveliest stops in South America. Anchored around a large Atlantic harbor, Montevideo is a city of the sea and summer.

Many in the small Mennonite community in Uruguay came originally from Danzig, Prussia — now Gdansk, Poland — over 50 years ago. A shipload of Mennonites arrived by sea from Europe in 1948. Seven hundred and fifty-five of these displaced persons stayed in Uruguay. The rest moved on to Paraguay. While sharing many of the names of Mennonites whose history wove through Russia, the German-speaking Uruguayan immigrants have a history which does not include the Russian experience, and they do not speak Low German, which is the first language of most of the German Mennonites in Paraguay who came out of Russia. The Uruguayan Mennonites connect more directly to the country of Germany, and not just the German language.

There are also a small number of Spanish-speaking Mennonites in Uruguay. Pastor Hugo Moreira offers a friendly entrée to his beautiful, pasto-ral country and to the church community.

Spanish and German congregations share a church in Montevideo that includes housing for students from Mennonite colonies who come to the city to attend university. Günter and Doris Meckelburger are members of the German church. They are retired dairy farmers who in recent years moved to the city to be closer to medical care for Doris' then severe back problems and so that she could pursue her interest in art nearer to other artists. Doris uses her maiden name Haak when signing her artwork. Expanding her artistic outlet later in life has steered her into more independent territory.

The Meckelburgers live in a modest but comfortable row house in a quiet neighborhood in Montevideo. They enjoy doing their shopping for meat, fish, fruit and vegetables at street markets which are set up on different residential streets on different days of each week, returning the same day the following week. A few drab blocks flower into a colorful and active spread on the day when the market comes. One sprouts up each week near their home.

At every opportunity children play football (soccer) on the street in front of the Meckelburger's residence. These games seem to be as much a part of

life's rhythm as the markets and the near-constant barking of dogs nearby and farther away during the night. It is quiet for a moment, then one dog yelps weakly, likely at nothing in particular, but this bark triggers another, then another. Eventually all the dogs for blocks around decide something terrible must be happening, so they all accelerate into frantic woofing and howling. Gradually the yelping tapers off, and it's quiet. Then a single bark, and they are off again on the same cycle.

In retirement Günter has taken on household responsibilities. Doris cooks. Günter cleans up and does the dishes. They tried the opposite, but did not like the results. Doris' first love is to go to a community studio shared with other artists to work on her ceramics. Günter loves the countryside and revels in driving out to the Mennonite retreat at Cuchilla Alta. The retreat was built on beachfront property purchased by three German congregations a number of years ago. The two-storey building is about 100 meters through bush to a sand cliff overlooking a long sweep of Atlantic beach. The building can house small conferences and church gatherings, and it can provide sleeping accommodations for up to 40 persons. People can also camp on the grounds. The wide, long sandy beach beckons bathers in the summer.

Uruguayans, like Brazilians, Paraguayans and Argentineans, are great lovers of beef. Old Montevideo is home to the Old Port Market, essentially a giant barbeque pit — restaurant after restaurant with huge, blazing fires, and grills stacked with thick, juicy cuts of beef. The air is filled with smoke from the fires, and with talk and laughter. It is a beef lovers' paradise.

Barbequing is also an essential part of Cuchilla Alta, the retreat center. A place for barbequing is built into the building. After a quick look round to make sure all is well, setting up the barbeque is always Günter's first priority. As large iguanas sun on nearby stones, slabs of beef sizzle delectably on the grill. The Atlantic breeze cools the seaside air, but this doesn't stop a swim from being part of the day's menu. Cuchilla Alta is a lovely spot.

Back in Montevideo, the Spanish congregation in the building where the Meckelburgers attend the German service is led by Hermann Woelke. He is also a chaplain at the Evangelico Hospital. Woelke is a Uruguayan of Danzig Mennonite heritage. He is equally at home in the Spanish Uruguayan community. Hermann's wife, Amalia, is a Spanish Paraguayan. She runs a counseling service from their home at the Mennonite Center. Both Hermann and Amalia are gentle, warm and friendly. Obviously their hearts are with their congregation. Their 20-year-old daughter is involved with the music in the church. Church responsibilities are a family affair.

Christmas is in summer in Uruguay, which allowed the Christmas program at Woelke's church to be staged in two places simultaneously, one inside and the other out of doors, when I visited them. A Spanish drama took place in the front. The manger scene, with kids and adults, was set up outside, just beyond a glass wall and large glass doors. The pageant went on for two hours. All the lines in the play — geared towards outreach to the general community — were memorized by the partici- pating congregation members. All the lines that is, except those of the wise men. They managed to cheat by taping their lines onto the tops of their gifts. At times they appeared to be studying their gifts with great intensity and squinting, depending on the shifting light and shadows. The pageant was followed by a full banquet that did not begin until nearly 11 p.m. King Herod could speak English fluently and was asked to sit with me and a group of teenagers. It was a celebration. The room was filled to overflowing and included young and old and members' friends and families invited for the special occasion. The community spirit was high.

Günter and Doris feel that the strength of Uruguay's German Mennonites is their devotion to community. They fear their small group is shrinking, and they are apprehensive about the move toward more generically evangelical beliefs by the younger members. They may thus lose their attachment to their community and its roots, the

(opposite) The beach at Cuchilla Alta. (above) Teens at a church Christmas banquet. (right) Children playing in front of the home of Doris and Günter Meckelburger.

very things which Doris and Günter find to be their safety and comfort.

Four years ago the Meckelburger's 18-year-old granddaughter, Katia, was killed by a drunk driver. The passing years have not eased the pain for Doris and Günter, especially since it was a hit-and-run accident and the perpetrator has not been identified. It was known that there were witnesses to the accident, but police requests for them to come forward resulted in nothing. A photo of Katia on the Meckelburger's living room shelves still moves Doris to tears.

Katia was buried at the Mennonite cemetery at Delta Colony, parallel to the Rio de la Plata, a 90 minute drive west of Montevideo.

Günter and Doris drove me to

At Delta Colony. (left) Elder Wolfram Driedger leads a baptismal service. (above) In the colony village.

Delta for a baptism. Delta has about 140 residents, with a cluster of buildings at its core ringed by scattered dairy farms and beekeeping operations. This was to be the first baptism by immersion in the tiny community. Only recently baptismal candidates were offered the choice as to whether they wished to be immersed or sprinkled. The church is now open to either mode.

On a splendid summer day, the members of Delta colony gathered near a small pond in a rich emerald dip below Elder Wolfram Driedger's farmhouse. People sat in lawn chairs. A small choir sang. It was led by a woman in blue jeans who played a guitar. The elder led the service. We moved to the pond for the baptism. While the young man entered the water the congregation sang softly. Lily pads swayed inside indigo ripples. Lime green parrots darted through trees behind the pond. Cows grazed in the lush pasture up the gentle incline behind us. The blue sky was brilliant. A tiny community grew by one.

Günter and Doris drove to the colony's center — a tiny, tranquil village — for lunch at a friend's home. On the way they stopped outside the cemetery. They took small garden tools and a few flowers out of the trunk of the car and silently passed through the wrought iron gate into the cemetery. They paused to look at the graves of their parents. Then quietly tended the grave of their beloved granddaughter for a long time, but it probably never seems long enough.

A Sunday at Delta colony. (clockwise from top) Inside the church; at the baptismal service; Günter and Doris Meckelburger lunch with friends.

(opposite) Waiting outside a church in Montevideo. Art by Roberto Cadenas (top) and Juan Mastromatteo (bottom). (this page) Painting by Luis Haro.

surface area: 9,976,140 sq. km.
capital: Ottawa
population: 31.5 million (2003)
language: English, French
religion: Catholic 43%, Protestants 32%, Orthodox 1.6%, Muslim 2%, Jewish 1.1%, Buddhist 1%, Hindu 1%, Sikh .9%, No religion 16.2%
literacy: 97%
life expectancy: 77 (men), 82 (women)
annual income per capita: US $21,930

United Nations Human Development Index: 8 out of 175 countries (2003)

Canada

Mennonite World Conference
Member Churches

Name: Canadian Conference of Mennonite Brethren Churches (The)
Local churches: 225
Members: 34,864

Name: Evangelical Mennonite Conference
Local churches: 49
Members: 7,068

Name: Evangelical Mennonite Mission Conference (US and Canada)
Local churches: 32
Members: 4,391

Name: Mennonite Church Canada
Local churches: 250
Members: 37,000

Gift Highlights: Educational institutions, religious books and publishing network, business and entrepreneurial expertise, musicians and artists, health professionals

Canada

Calgary
Winnipeg
Ottawa
Vancouver
Montreal
Toronto
Kitchener-Waterloo

family stories

On July 19, 2003, Agatha Reimer marked a century on this earth. She has lived peacefully in Winnipeg since the 1950s. The first half of her life, however, was punctuated by periods of turmoil, hardships and horror. As a teenager growing up in southern Russia she experienced the Russian Revolution. The Communist revolt uprooted and traumatized many Mennonites. These German-speaking people, many of whom were Christians and who lived in close communities and were often successful farmers and businesspeople, became easy targets of the revolutionary forces. In the 1920s many of them fled to North America. Others stayed, hoping for better times in Russia. The madness of the dictator Josef Stalin ensured that those hopes would never be realized.

Agatha's husband, Gerhard, was arrested in 1937. A final meeting was allowed, and Agatha, accompanied by her youngest son, Abram, traveled to the prison. Over 65 years later Abram still vividly recalls the tears in both his parents' eyes as their closely monitored visit ended. Gerhard died — as did millions of others — under the ruthless and paranoid rule of Stalin. In 1943, with only two men left in their village, Agatha and a group of other women and children decided to flee during the chaos of World War II.

Winter closed in as they headed up through the Ukraine and into Poland. Shoes disintegrated in the mud and snow. They pushed on. They ran out of food. Sons were forced into the retreating German army. They pushed on. Agatha often prayed, pleading to God, "We are at our end. What can we do?" They crossed Poland into Germany and became stuck in Berlin at the end of the war. They feared repatriation to Russia — 23,000 out of 35,000 fleeing Mennonites were sent back to a life of persecution and misery.

Agatha and two of her three sons hid with others in bombed-out homes in Berlin. Rumors of their existence reached Peter J. Dyck of the Mennonite Central Committee. He journeyed to Berlin, found them and helped them to eventually escape from Berlin through the Russian sector of postwar Germany to Bremerhaven where they boarded the Dutch ship, the Volendam, for South America. The Mennonite refugees wished to join the established Mennonite communities in Canada, but they were denied entry after World War II. Paraguay welcomed them mostly as settlers in the forbidding Chaco region.

Life in the arid, dust-drenched Chaco was difficult for Agatha and the other Mennonite pioneers. The greatest joy was that her third son was able to find out that his brothers and mother had gone to Paraguay and he managed to reunite with them there.

Canada remained the hoped-for promised land, and in the early 1950s

Agatha Reimer, who lives at a Mennonite personal care home, Donwood Manor, in Winnipeg. She turned 100 on July 19, 2003.

Agatha was sponsored by a sister in Winnipeg to move north. Her three sons eventually followed, and all of them settled in North Kildonan, an area of Winnipeg still with a high concentration of German-speaking Mennonites with roots in Russia and the Ukraine.

Canada is a land of immigrants and refugees. A 2001 study revealed that 18.4% of the residents in this country were born outside of Canada, the second highest percentage in the world, after Australia. Toronto, Canada's largest city, listed 44% of its population as being born in a different nation. Up to 1960 most immigrants to Canada came from Europe. In recent decades that changed, with influxes from China, India and other Asian countries leading the way. Vancouver, Canada's beautiful third city, now boasts a population that is approximately 50% nonwhite. A large suburb to the south of Vancouver, Richmond, is now 60% visible minority. Mennonite churches are trying to catch up and reflect the diversity of the country.

Jane Zheng did not hear about Christianity until 1980 during her second year at university. In China, where she grew up, information about religion and the outside world was actively suppressed. While in university in her homeland she heard Bible stories on an overseas shortwave radio station. They intrigued her but her belief in the theory of evolution stopped her from becoming anything more than vaguely interested. She couldn't get past the first chapter of Genesis.

In 1991 Jane's husband, Yongsheng Ye, moved to Winnipeg to study for his PhD at the University of Manitoba. Jane and their son, Peng Ye, followed in 1993. She brought two suitcases, thinking her time in Canada would be

Young parishioners in the Winnipeg Chinese Mennonite Church. (right) Jane Zheng at the office. She works in the finance department of Mennonite Church Canada in Winnipeg.

brief.

Upon arriving she noticed that Canada was different than what she had been taught in China. The freedom available to everyone impressed her most. She decided to stay and continue her studies in Canada. Unable to gain entry into University in Manitoba, Jane moved to Edmonton to study at the University of Alberta for two years. Living apart was not a big issue for either Yongsheng or Jane. In China it is common for couples to live in different cities for years because of the study or work of one or the other.

After returning to Winnipeg Jane looked for a piano teacher for Peng Ye. Since she was not yet fluent in English, she searched for and found a Chinese Canadian teacher. He happened to be the pastor of the Winnipeg Chinese Mennonite Church. Peng Ye learned to play the piano. Jane learned more about the Bible. Her earlier spark of interest from her university days in China was rekindled. Through her discussions with the piano teacher she became a Christian and began to attend the Winnipeg Chinese Mennonite Church.

The Winnipeg Chinese Mennonite Church is mostly made up of immigrants who have arrived in Canada in recent years from mainland China, Taiwan and Hong Kong. Services are conducted in Mandarin or Cantonese, often with English translation. Many of the children are already more familiar with English than the Chinese languages, making translation to English necessary.

There are a growing number of Mennonite churches in Canada now serving recently arrived communities from places such as China, Vietnam, Laos, South Korea and Latin America. Many of the long-established Mennonite churches now find their growth coming from the general community rather than from those people who grew up in

Caili Woodyard, seated to the left, and Heather Block, standing second from right, with people who frequent the Andrews Street Family Centre. The center is located in one of the poorest neighborhoods in Canada. Block, a member of nearby Aberdeen Evangelical Mennonite Church, is program director. Woodyard, from Ottawa, is a Mennonite Central Committee volunteer at the center.

families with long histories in Mennonite churches reaching back to Russia, the Ukraine, Prussia, Switzerland or the Netherlands. Where once Mennonites in North America could almost all be identified by their last names, that is no longer the case in many churches and communities.

But so-called "ethnic" Mennonites are still found in great numbers in Winnipeg and in surrounding towns, especially to the south of the city towards the US border. Southern Manitoba has long been dominated by Mennonite businesses and farms. The people of the region have a reputation as being successful, hard working and generous. Steinbach, a town with a large Mennonite population, statistically is the most charitable community in Canada.

Agatha Reimer does have a last name that has long been equated with being Mennonite. To her the word Mennonite implies Christianity and also the language, food and culture with which she is familiar. To Jane Zheng and a growing number of members the word Mennonite is simply attached to the church she attends. Both new and old should be at home within the church.

Agatha looks back on her long years and remembers the pain of losing a husband and home in Europe, of struggle in Paraguay, of losing a second husband in Canada. She also rejoices in having lived a good life with family around her in Canada. The invitation to her 100th birthday celebration at the Mennonite personal care home where she lives proclaimed: "Celebrating 100 years of God's goodness." A Bible verse followed: "Even to your old age and gray hairs I am He, I am He who will sustain you. I have made you and I will carry you." (Isaiah 46:4)

Scenes from a memorable summer. (this page) Relatives gather for the 19th birthday party of Lauren Dirks. (opposite page) Lauren and other baptismal candidates in the water at Bird's Hill Provincial Park outside Winnipeg and with her proud mother, Katie, after being baptized.

Turn the page: (top) Jubilee Mennonite Church's congregation comes together for a baptism. Retired missionary Abe Rempel relaxes in his lawn chair before the baptism begins. (below left) Lauren Dirks takes communion for the first time after her baptism. (below right) Worship leader Rob Mitchell leads singing at the service. Mitchell is also a member of the Christian rock group Freeman.

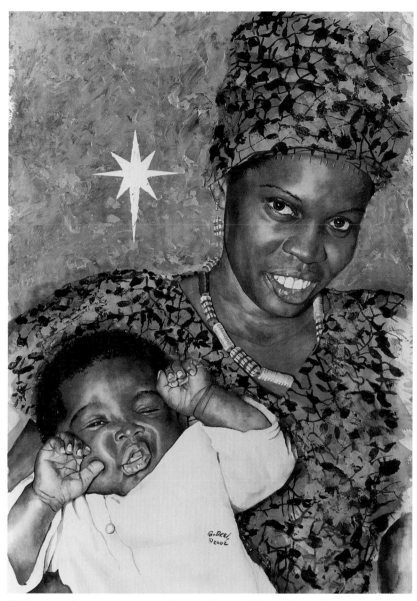

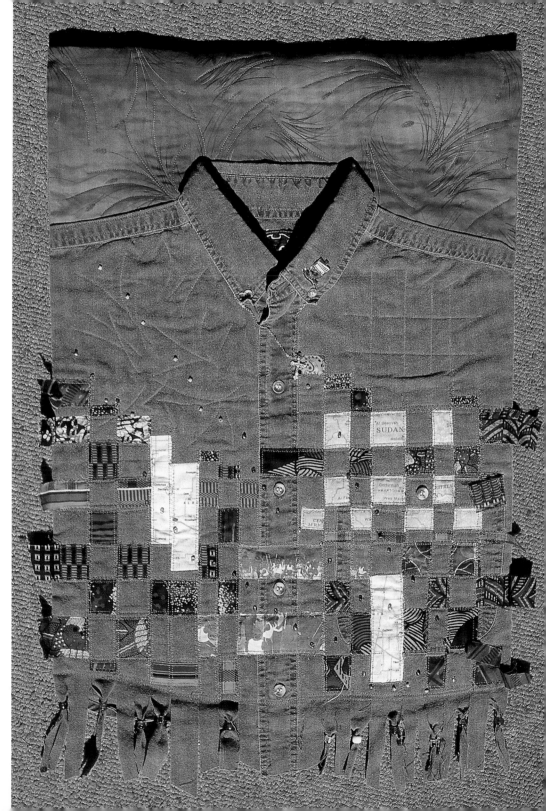

(left) Painting by Ray Dirks of a Sudanese refugee and her child, now living in Winnipeg, symbolizing the Madonna and Christ child.

(right) Strangers no More by Alberta's Ruth Bergen Braun. Fabric artist Braun was inspired to create this artwork after 1,000 Sudanese refugees were recruited by a local meat packing plant to move into her Alberta town of 12,000. Braun incorporated bits of African cloth, maps and photos into the piece.

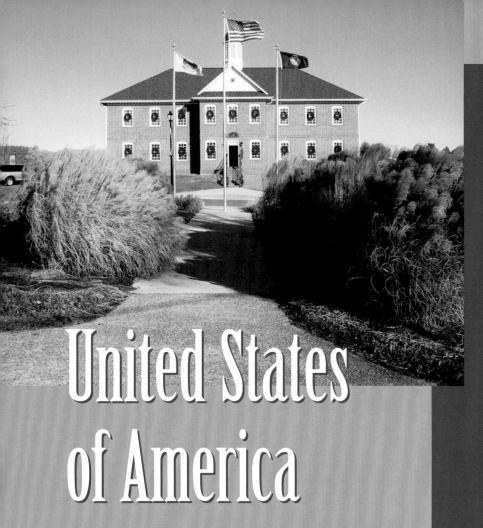

United States of America

surface area: 9,826,675 sq. km.
capital: Washington, DC
population: 291 million (2003)
language: English, Spanish
major religion: Protestant 61%,
Catholic 25%, Jewish 2%, other 5%,
none 7%
literacy: 97%
life expectancy: 74 (men), 80 (women)
annual income per capita: US $34,280

United Nations Human Development
Index: 7 out of 175 countries (2003)

Mennonite World Conference
Member Churches

Name: Conservative Mennonite
Conference
Local churches: 106
Members: 10,429

Name: Mennonite Church USA
Local churches: 980
Members: 110,252

Name: U.S. Conference of Mennonite
Brethren Churches
Local churches: 188
Members: 26,219

CANADA/USA
Name: Brethren in Christ General
Conference (North America)
Local churches: 274
Members: 24,162

Gift Highlights: Teaching skills in
conflict management, Anabaptist
Historians, health professionals,
mission and service organizations,
educational institutions

(above) The American flag, a venerated symbol in a country charged by patriotism.

(opposite) In the Pennsylvania Mennonite heartland.

family stories stories

Early Anabaptist history bulges with stories of persecution and relocation. In early 16th century Europe church and state were closely knit. By law infants had to be baptized, becoming part of the church and requiring parents to pay church taxes for each child. The founders of the Anabaptist movement felt church and state should be separate and that people should decide themselves whether or not they would be part of the church — being baptized at an age when the person can make his or her own decision as opposed to automatically as an infant. In 1525 a small group gathered together in Zurich, Switzerland for Bible study. They decided to baptize one another. They became known as the Anabaptists (re-baptizers). Martyrdom followed for many.

Roaming Europe looking for places where they would be allowed to live and believe as they wished in peace also followed. Eventually some gazed west across the ocean.

Jan Lensen arrived on North American shores in October 1683, becoming the first Mennonite in what was to become the United States of America. He settled along with some German Quaker families north of Philadelphia. Germantown was born and other European Mennonites followed soon after. Pennsylvania became the home of many Mennonites, first enticed there by William Penn's offer of religious freedom. Pennsylvania has remained home to a large number of Mennonites ever since.

Freedom to live and worship as they believed was directed by God led to a large influx of Mennonites to North America beginning in the 1870s. Kansas, Nebraska and South Dakota were opening up and farmers were needed. The passing of a law by the Kansas legislature granting exemption from compulsory National Guard duty gave German-speaking Mennonites confidence to uproot from Russia. Known as followers of a path of peace and nonresistance, guarantees of exemption from military service were important. About 100 years earlier Catherine the Great had invited Mennonites to Russia to farm newly acquired territory gained after defeating the Turks. With Catherine's passing her promise to the Mennonites to protect them from military draft began to be ignored. Mennonites again began to search for new homes. The plains of the US and Canada beckoned.

Eventually Mennonites spread all across the US, with significant concentrations in, to name a few states, Pennsylvania, Kansas, Indiana, Ohio and California. US Mennonites share a common faith

LANDIS HOMES
Retirement Community

WEST ENTRANCE

1001 East Oregon Road

at its core but there is a great diversity of belief and practice beyond the central Christian basics. For example, while still having a reputation for standing for pacifism it is by no means a universally held position. Many American Mennonites feel uncomfortable with their government's absolute determination to maintain global military superiority and willingness to pursue peace and national interest through war, but many have also embraced the thinking and wishes of presidents such as Ronald Reagan and George W. Bush.

Diversity stretches beyond opinions of how to live as Christians in the most powerful nation on earth. A community once exclusively of European heritage is no longer such. There are Mennonite churches representing many more recently arrived communities and ones within the US's longstanding African American community.

Andrew Schrock, 22, grew up in the region where the Mennonites first settled in the United States. Lancaster, Pennsylvania, is home. Karina Derksen, 21, meanwhile, was born and raised far from the US but in another area with a large concentration of Mennonites. Her parents were missionaries with Africa Inter-Mennonite Mission at the time of her birth at Kalonda, Zaire (now Democratic Republic of Congo). Except for one year in Canada, she lived in Zaire until 1998, when her family moved to Pennsylvania. The change of address led to a change of schools from one in Kinshasa with students from all over the world to the Lancaster Mennonite High School. Karina missed the diversity of her previous school but came to appreciate getting to know others in Pennsylvania from similar backgrounds and with similar beliefs to hers. This, along with a natural people-oriented character, helped her adjust quickly to her new environment.

While Karina's life wove its way about the world Andrew's stayed in Lancaster. Their paths intersected in their junior year of high school. Both were in the spring musical, *My Fair Lady*. Their meeting was no epiphany — no fireworks went off.

During their senior year they were both part of the same group of friends. As a result, they began to get to know one another. After high school they parted ways, going to different colleges. But they kept in some contact during their school breaks back in Lancaster. Andrew moved to London for a semester and he and Karina began to send e-mails back and forth. The greater distance between them served to bring them closer together and a special relationship started while they were farthest apart. Andrew recalls that for every e-mail he sent, Karina sent at least two. He became impressed by her devotion to family and friends.

(opposite) Bob and Alta Ranck, retired and living in the Landis Homes Retirement Community. Landis Homes is a full-service, continuing care Mennonite retirement community on a rural 100-acre campus in Lititz, Pennsylvania.

That devotion and strength of character which so impresses Andrew carries over to Karina's faith walk. She is passionate about her faith and about ideals that are important to her — such as pacifism and standing up for social justice. She knows what she believes and is not afraid to defend her beliefs.

Andrew says that growing up in a community where there is a strong, ethnically identified Mennonite presence obscured to him what it means to be Mennonite. "Being a Mennonite is something that has become important to me. I was not always sure of what it meant to be Mennonite. Although my family is Mennonite, my church is Mennonite, and I went to a Mennonite high school, I did not understand what Mennonites represented," relates Andrew.

Leaving Lancaster to go to college elsewhere brought Andrew into contact with people who, like Karina, see being Mennonite as being a follower of Christ who promotes a challenging lifestyle that in many ways is contrary to popular culture. Andrew now says, "Though I do not want to put myself into too much of a denominational box by labeling myself as a Mennonite, I agree with the theological distinctives of Mennonites — pacifism, adult baptism, emphasis on community and simple lifestyle, and social awareness."

Karina and Andrew's relationship recently evolved into engagement and a desire to spend their lives together in service. They don't know where they will be led. Andrew's intention is to continue on to medical school. Karina wants a career that will point to helping others in the wider world, perhaps through working with a non-governmental organization or church agency overseas. Both enjoy church, family and friends in Pennsylvania, but they do not think their long-term futures will be found there.

Andrew and Karina are just beginning their lives together. Werner and Elsie Ann Kroeker have spent more than 50 years devoted to one another and their church. Werner was born in South Dakota and Elsie Ann in Oklahoma. They now make their home in Fresno. Werner was a pastor from 1954 to 1993. From 1993 to 2000, when they retired to California, the Kroekers spent most of their time in India working as liaisons between the Mennonite Brethren churches in India and North America. Their enthusiasm for the global family of faith as reflected through Mennonite World Conference (MWC) is inspiring. Their love, positive attitude, humility and gentle spirit speak well of their personal integrity.

Werner speaks passionately about the worldwide church, "The center has moved to the global South, the growth is there, we have much to learn from what God has been doing among our people there and we have an opportunity to continue to share with them what God has given us. What we really are, what we most are, is often more obvious to others than it is to us. In our interaction with and relationship to the church in other parts of the world, we will come to better understand our own need and our own potential. We in

North America and Europe need to see ourselves as aging parents of mature children in the churches of Africa, Asia and Latin America."

Anabaptist Christians began journeying to the US more than 300 years ago. From its fortunate shores many have since set out across oceans and boundaries to work for the church, to increase the global family of faith, to help as doctors, nurses and educators, to stand shoulder to shoulder with ordinary people in troubled lands as active nonresistant peacemakers, to aid in creating small businesses, to bring food in time of famine. Now it is also up to North America to accept counsel and wisdom from distant shores where people from the US have often helped to start and nourish the global Anabaptist family.

This prospect excites Werner and Elsie Ann. It invigorates Andrew and Karina, too. They attended the Assembly Gathered of MWC in Bulawayo, Zimbabwe in August 2003. They participated as youth stewards, a group of

university-age young adults from several countries who came together to get to know each other, and through each other the global church, and to help put together the Global Village exhibition at the assembly. Back home in Lancaster, Karina reflects, "Through working with MWC, I have become increasingly interested in working with the Mennonite church and learning more about the global family of faith."

Honorable lives lived and being lived by people like Werner and Elsie Ann and lives to be lived in the hope of sharing with, helping and receiving from the global family of faith by people like Andrew and Karina evidence there are many reasons to be thankful for the tiny community Jan Lensen helped found in Germantown more than three centuries ago.

all photos these two pages by Scott Jost, Harrisonburg, Virginia

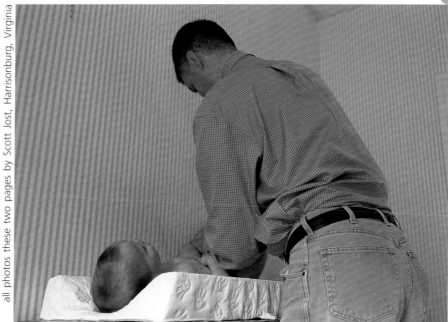

(both pages) John Swartzentruber, his wife Lauren McKinney and their boys Jack and Will. Swartzentruber and McKinney attend the Community Mennonite Church in Harrisonburg, Virginia. John is a software developer who telecommutes for a company in Ohio. Lauren taught at Eastern Mennonite University and is now mostly a stay-at-home mom although she does some freelance writing and editing. These photos, by Virginia photographer Scott Jost, show a daily life with both parents very involved in their children's lives.

(top) Virginia photographer/professor Scott Jost's photographs of an apple orchard in the Shenandoah Valley. (left) Doug Dirks of Ten Thousand Villages, an organization helping thousands of artisans in the global South find markets for their crafts, in Akron, Pennsylvania. (above) On the grounds of the Mennonite Central Committee (MCC) in Akron.

(above left) Artist and art professor at Eastern Mennonite University Barbara Fast. (above) Handmade paper art by Barbara Fast. (left) At MCC in Akron. MCC is a relief, service and peace agency of Mennonite and Brethren in Christ churches. The grounds and buildings in Akron reflect a sensitivity towards and an identification with the people around the world with which MCC works.

France

surface area: 547,030 sq. km.
capital: Paris
population: 60.1 million (2003)
language: French
major religion: Catholic 81%,
Protestant 1.7%, Muslim 6.9%,
Jewish 1.3%
literacy: 99%
life expectancy: 75 (men), 83
(women)
annual income per capita: US
$22,730

United Nations Human Development Index:
17 out of 175 countries (2003)

Mennonite World Conference
Member Church

Name: Association des Eglises Evangéliques
Mennonites de France
Local churches: 30
Members: 2,050

Switzerland

surface area: 41,290 sq. km.
capital: Bern
population: 7.1 million (2003)
language: German, French, Italian, Romansch
major religion: Catholic 49%, Protestant 40%, other 5%, no religion
8.3%
literacy: 99%
life expectancy: 76 (men), 82 (women)
annual income per capita: US $38,330

United Nations Human Development Index:
10 out of 175 countries (2003)

Mennonite World Conference Member Church

Name: Konferenz der Mennoniten der Schweiz (Alttäufer)/Conférence
Mennonite Suisse (Anabaptiste)
Local churches: 14
Members: 2,500

Gift Highlights: Theological training institution, religious
literature, Anabaptist historians and theologians

Vikings! They ate brains! Why didn't the Vikings tell Christopher Columbus that they had arrived in North America centuries before he did? Raphäel Wiedmer has come home from school obsessed with Vikings.

Raphäel is the middle child of Max and Astrid Wiedmer who live in Altkirch, France. He is a joy to behold, an eager and inquisitive child whose imagination is not yet bound by pretense or possible embarrassment. Life is wonderful and exciting. A class on Vikings has made a tremendous impression on him and sent his imagination soaring into a world of fact, fiction and fancy. All evening the Norsemen of old are worked into his every conversation.

The Wiedmers make a habit of having breakfast together. They begin with family devotions. A night's sleep has not dislodged the Vikings from Raphäel's thoughts. Max begins reading the Easter story. Somehow Raphäel works the Vikings into the resurrection account. Might they have been there? The entire family — his parents, his older brother Alexandre and his younger sister Salomé — begin to laugh. They cannot stop. Finally Max closes his Bible and says, "We will have devotions at dinner."

Max and Astrid head a family filled with love — one where spending time together, being a family regardless of how busy life may become, is not an option but essential. Both parents are deeply involved in the lives of their children. Their children know how much they are loved. Being a child in the family does, however, come with responsibilities. Each is required to work around the home. Each takes many lessons outside of school — in music, sports, and dance for Salomé. There is discipline in how they live, as is illustrated in their devotional, home and extracurricular lives.

The children go to school Monday, Tuesday, Thursday and Friday, from 8:30 to 11:30 a.m. in the morning and 1:00 to 4:45 p.m. in the afternoon. They also go every other Saturday morning.

In the Alsace area, which borders Switzerland and Germany, the Swiss German language was once commonly used and is known by Max and Astrid. Now, however, most of the children wish to know and speak only French. Those who know Swiss German speak an accented French, an accent which is sometimes made fun of in school.

Max and Astrid were born in France and grew up in the Birkenhof Mennonite Church in the Alsace countryside. They are French, but their family roots are in Switzerland. Max works across the border in Switzerland. He owns a video production company, Affox, in Allschwil, a suburb of the beautiful city of Basel. He also works at the Ausbildungs- und Tagungszentrum Bienenberg, formerly called the European Mennonite Bible School. Bienenberg is in a lovely setting, perched on top of a small mountain, with the town of Liestal spread out below.

Opposite: (top) Beautiful Strasbourg, home of the main office of Mennonite World Conference. (bottom) The restored Basel city hall.

(above) Zurich, Switzerland

Max's route to Switzerland follows roads Napoleon built along the spines of hills so his army could see all around as they moved. Hills fall away on both sides into low valleys as the road winds towards the border. Bunkers along the Maginot Line built to stop the advancing German army in World War II are a regular sight. The border is crossed without stopping. Max needs to weave his vehicle slightly, forcing him to slow down to pass the border post. The guards barely look up, if at all, and Max continues on to work.

The road to Bienenberg heads more into back country than the one to Basel. Narrow roads lead through forests and past farms. At one point a narrow, steep climb leads past a small castle, seemingly in the middle of nowhere. It is on a wooded promontory overlooking a lonely pasture with an old bathtub as a trough for the animals.

Astrid and Max still attend the Birkenhof church. This congregation has a daughter church in Altkirch, but the Wiedmers continue to go to the country church they have known all their lives. The church was built near a cluster of five Mennonite farms, only two of which are still owned by Mennonites. Five elders oversee the two churches, three at Birkenhof and two at Altkirch. Birkenhof has about 180 members and Altkirch 50. Neither church has a paid pastor. Elders are unpaid and serve for life. Each French church is independent and need not follow what others or the majority of others do or wish among the 31 Mennonite churches in France. Four churches have women elders.

A two-hour drive from Max and Astrid's home into Switzerland and following near the French border leads to La Chaux de Fonds in the French-speaking sector of multilingual Switzerland. In the early days of the Swiss Anabaptists they were not allowed to farm below 1,000 meters. La Chaux de Fonds is situated on a plateau high enough so that the Mennonites were allowed to settle and work the land. The climb up to the plateau and the road along its crest fits extraordinarily well into a Swiss stereotype. Everything seems perfect. It appears one is driving through a park, everything flawlessly manicured and in order, the towns quaint and pretty in beautiful rolling mountain settings. This is not the Alps but it is scenic nonetheless. Tiny one-car trains traverse the plateau. The area is a bit off the beaten path. The large, sophisticated trains are down below speeding to cities like Zurich, Geneva, Luzern and Basel. La Chaux de Fonds is removed from that bustle.

Vitrail, stained glass, artist Marguerite Gerber Geiser and her husband Joël live in La Chaux de Fonds. They reside in one of the many uniform apartment buildings which are several floors high. They live on the top floor. The old building has no elevator. The long climb helps to keep the people at the top in

The spot in Zurich where Felix Manz became the first Anabaptist martyr, drowned for his faith.

shape. Marguerite and Joël both come across as gentle and sensitive. Joël is a great supporter of his wife as an artist. A gifted craftsman with wood, Joël often puts the finishing touches on Marguerite's work, contributing handmade frames to her glass artworks.

Marguerite keeps a studio downtown. It is full of fine handmade glass pieces in various colors. She is very careful to use good materials. Marguerite is not only a talented artist but also a careful technician, making sure each artwork is not only creative but of the best quality. She often takes biblical stories and scenes and gives them a contemporary look. Her interpretation and style make something old seem fresh and new.

Marguerite and Joël are from longtime Swiss Mennonite families. They can trace their roots back generations. They attend Les Bulles church outside La Chaux de Fonds. It is surrounded by Mennonite farms in a typical, traditional setup. The church is a simple building. Entering it feels like coming into a cottage. The entrance is small, and the floor and the walls immediately inside the door are all wood. The sanctuary is upstairs. It, too, is not ostentatious. But there is one flourish. At the front of the sanctuary there are four beautiful stained glass windows, two on each side.

The windows were commissioned by a member of the church. Marguerite is thankful for the support she has found in her church family. Each week, for as long as this congregation will gather in this place of worship, her witness will shine for all to see and to contemplate. The windows help point people towards worship in a way that confirms the ability to interpret visually is certainly a gift from God which the church should embrace.

Descending from the plateau, away from the toy-like trains, regular fast trains speed people to the core of early Anabaptism in Switzerland. Zurich is a modern, sophisticated lakeside city. A walk into the small, quiet side streets of the old city, winding away from the 21st century, retraces the steps of early Anabaptism. There's the church and home of Ulrich Zwingli, and there's Conrad Grebel's home. Down by the river below the cathedral, near the lake, is the spot where Felix Manz became the first Anabaptist martyr, drowned for his faith. Would I have the strength to do that?

There are plenty of exciting stories from the early days of the Anabaptists, of adventure and bravery, of loyalty and putting faith ahead of security — such as that of Dutchman Dirk Willems who turned back to save the life of his pursuer who had fallen through the ice, which then resulted in his being captured and killed. These stories rival those of the Vikings for excitement, and they come with a message of sacrifice and faith as opposed to plunder and pillage. Raphäel could get excited about these, too, and work them more easily into the family devotions.

(top right) Bienenberg Bible school and retreat center above the Swiss town of Liestal near Basel. (bottom right) Retired women from the Mennonite church in Montbéliard, France, volunteer to help with renovations at Bienenberg.

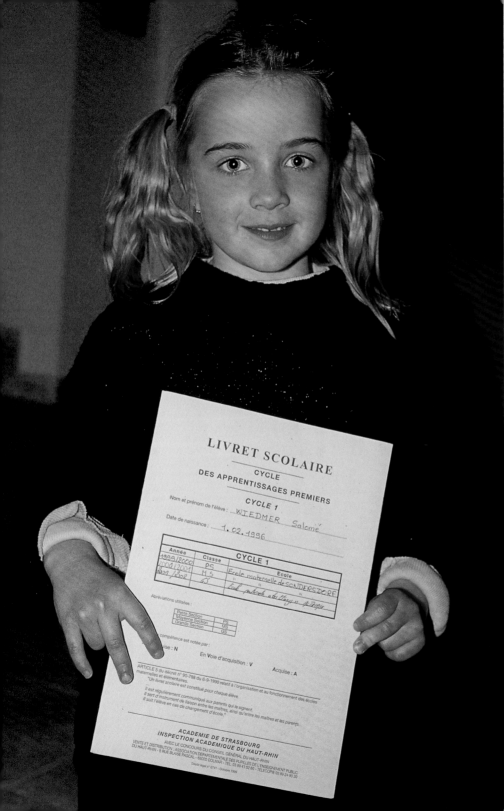

LIVRET SCOLAIRE

CYCLE

DES APPRENTISSAGES PREMIERS

CYCLE 1

Nom et prénom de l'élève : WIEDMER Salomé

Date de naissance : 1.02.1996

Année	Classe	CYCLE 1
		École
1999/2000	PS	
2000/2001	MS	École maternelle de SONDERSDORF
2001/2002	GS	

Abréviations utilisées :

Petite Section	PS
Moyenne Section	MS
Grande Section	GS

...compétence est notée par :

...use : N   En Voie d'acquisition : V   Acquise : A

ARTICLE 5 du décret n° 90-788 du 6-9-1990 relatif à l'organisation et au fonctionnement des écoles maternelles et élémentaires.

"Un livret scolaire est constitué pour chaque élève.

Il est régulièrement communiqué aux parents qui le signent.

Il sert d'instrument de liaison entre les maîtres, ainsi qu'entre les maîtres et les parents.

Il suit l'élève en cas de changement d'école."

ACADEMIE DE STRASBOURG
INSPECTION ACADEMIQUE DU HAUT-RHIN

AVEC LE CONCOURS DU CONSEIL GENERAL DU HAUT-RHIN
VENTE ET DISTRIBUTION : ASSOCIATION DEPARTEMENTALE DES PUPILLES DE L'ENSEIGNEMENT PUBLIC
DU HAUT-RHIN - 8 RUE BLAISE PASCAL - 68000 COLMAR - TEL. 03 89 41 52 60 - TELECOPIE 03 89 24 90 30

Dépôt légal n° 6741 - Octobre 1999

Opposite: (clockwise from left) Salomé Wiedmer proudly shows her first grade report card. The new home of Astrid and Max Wiedmer in Altkirch, France. Salomé and Raphäel Wiedmer help out planting shrubs in their new yard.

This page: (clockwise from left) Astrid Wiedmer prepares to take the children to school. Max Wiedmer and assistant Eric Oberli set up for a video shoot outside the Basel cathedral overlooking the Rhine River. After family devotions the Wiedmers pray for their breakfast.

Max Wiedmer, left, and other elders oversee a baptism in the Birkenhof church.

(clockwise from left) Photograph by Claude Nardin, France. Marguerite Gerber Geiser at work in her studio. A stained glass artwork by Gerber Geiser. Les Bulles church near La Chaux de Fonds, Switzerland, where Gerber Geiser attends and has four stained glass windows.

surface area: 41,526 sq. km.
capital: Amsterdam
population: 16.1 million (2003)
language: Dutch , Frisian
major religion: Catholic 34%, Protestant 25%,
Muslim 3%, other 2%, unaffiliated 36%
literacy: 99%
life expectancy: 76 (men), 81 (women)
annual income per capita: US $24,330

United Nations Human Development Index:
5 out of 175 countries (2003)

Mennonite World Conference Member Church

Name: Algemene Doopsgezinde Sociëteit
Local churches: 123
Members: 11,000

Gift Highlights: Inter-church relations,
Anabaptist history resources, conflict
management, peace workers

Netherlands

"W hy," he asked, "does it seem most people who are members of Anabaptist churches in other countries know nothing about where their churches have their roots?" I had no answer for the Dutch Mennonite who was asking this question. There was confusion and a touch of sadness in his voice.

Anabaptism has roots leading back to more than one country in Europe, but the Netherlands is the most closely identified with this movement. It was the birthplace of Menno Simons more than 500 years ago, the man from whose name comes the word Mennonite. In a largely secular society, today's Dutch Mennonites are small in number — small, but sincere and active, especially in matters related to social issues.

Artist Annelies Soomers was not born into a Mennonite family. While teaching in Krommenie she became good friends with Janneke Hoekstra. Both women were going through difficult times in their lives. This deepened their bond of friendship. As well, they found unconditional support in Janneke's Mennonite church. Annelies also noted that the people of the church were actively involved in the cause of peace, the environment and justice for the oppressed. As a long-time supporter of Amnesty International, the conscience of the church drew her closer.

Annelies was so impressed by the integrity and values of the congregation that she decided she wanted to join. She saw them as guided by the example Christ lived in the Bible. She wanted to be part of such a community of followers of Christ. As a result she began attending the Doopsgezinde Gemeente Krommenie-Knollerdam, the Krommenie Mennonite Church. Eventually she asked to be baptized.

A baptismal candidate must write his or her own confession of faith and read it to the congregation in order to be baptized into the Dutch Mennonite community. The church is seen as the individuals who make up the membership of the community rather than as an institution. There is no institutional confession of faith. Each individual member, as a part of the church, is expected to have his or her own confession of faith. With that confession they are welcomed into the family of believers.

Krommenie is a small town about an hour's drive north of Amsterdam in a region of Holland where the fact that one is in a low country near the sea is ever apparent. Water seems to never be out of sight. Canals are everywhere. While driving on some roads along the tops of dikes the strange sensation, for a visitor at least, of having water on one side of the road higher than the farmland on the other can be a bit disconcerting.

The Krommenie Mennonite Church, like many older Dutch churches, does not look like a typical church. The first Anabaptists were hunted and killed. Having a church building was illegal. Eventually some churches were built behind houses, such as the Singel Church in Amsterdam, out of sight from the street. Then churches were allowed to be seen from the street, but they could not look like a church. The Krommenie church is from that period.

In 1702 a fire devastated Krommenie. Half the town was destroyed, including the Mennonite church. By May 1703 a new structure was in place. Annelies was commissioned to create a sculpture to commemorate the church's 300th birthday in May 2003. The church was restored to its original design for the anniversary.

From outside it is a plain but stately, deep green building on Krommenie's small main street. A simple side door leads into an entry area, a pleasant room that serves as a lobby to the sanctuary. The sanctuary is more or less square with a high ceiling, long windows and a balcony. There is an organ upstairs. The front of the sanctuary is dominated by a significant, dark wood pulpit. A tiny flight of stairs leads up to it. The inside of the church is neither grandiose nor totally simple. The floorboards are plain and unfinished. The pulpit and some of the flourishes in the ceiling and front of the balcony are quite ornate.

The floor is covered with a thin layer of very fine, raked-smooth sand. This comes out of a bygone necessity that has become an honored tradition. In times past boxes with hot coals were placed at the congregants' feet to keep them warm against winter's chill. The sand served as a barrier to protect the floor from catching fire.

Today people speak from behind a simple stand at the level of the congregation rather than climbing up behind the pulpit. A table with a large, centuries-old Bible is directly in front of them. The atmosphere is casual yet dignified. Whatever disagreement there may be between Dutch and some other Mennonites on issues of belief there is no disputing that their churches are the house of God.

As with many artists, Annelies wants her art to be somewhat provocative. It is not just pretty pictures. She believes that God asks us to be stewards of all His creation. To Annelies this means we must also cherish even the least of

(above) A daughter displays her mother's baptismal dress.

(left) A bicyclist glides past Ineke and Peter Reinhold's Amsterdam home.

living things. With this in mind, she created a series of drawings and paintings focusing on what most would term insignificant animals which are endangered. She believes fervently that they, too, should be saved and protected, that God watches not only how we treat each other but how we treat all of His nature.

Annelies lives with her husband René Walburgh Schmidt in the town of Bunnik, a ten-minute train ride from the city of Utrecht. Another short train jaunt beyond Utrecht ends at the central train station in Amsterdam.

Ineke and Peter Reinhold meet visitors to Amsterdam at the central station.

Inloophuis drop-in center in Almere. Ineke Reinhold talks to director Marjan Kip. Inloophuis is a mission project of the Dutch Mennonite Church.

them to remain in the city they love.

If a Mennonite visits Ineke and Peter, a trip to the Singel Church is a guarantee. Amsterdam's center is mostly buildings standing shoulder to shoulder up and down the full length of each block. There are many canals crossed by small bridges. Bicycles locked to canal fence railings line the bridges and waterways. The church is completely hidden from view behind what were three mid-block homes fronting a canal. The church, long since not having to be hidden, has a sign hanging at the street as the only way to tell from the outside that one has arrived. A long hall leads to the sanctuary. It is surprisingly large, seating up to 2,000, and has the appearance of an old concert hall with a huge pulpit at the front. Two levels of balconies ring three sides. The sense of history is palpable.

When Ineke took me into the sanctuary I did not want to leave. It was empty except for the two of us, but I felt the presence of so many before me. I could imagine voices in the balconies, words from behind the pulpit, people who in the early days of the Anabaptists chose a Christian path that was not easy. The Dutch Mennonites are doing their church work to this day, including mission projects such as the Inloophuis drop-in center in a poor, multi-ethnic area of Almere. For them, it is necessary to not be trapped in the past but to find and hold their place and relevance in the present.

I visited the Singel Church on the last day of the last trip for the *In God's Image* project. I had not set out to intentionally end the reference gathering in the country of Menno Simons. But the closer to the end of my travels it got the more appropriate it seemed to finish in a place so important in Anabaptist history. Ineke and I finally left the Singel Church sanctuary and headed down the long hall back to the door, the street, and the 21st century. I noted a long paper on the wall listing elders in the church. I followed it with my eyes. Then, in the first column, nearest the door, there was "Abram Dirks, 1617."

I have no idea whether or not I am a descendant of Abram Dirks — likely not. I have no idea if he accomplished much or little, or was simply ordinary. What struck me profoundly was that I am a part of a family with roots — roots in the soil of Menno Simons and in that of the martyrs of Switzerland and elsewhere in Europe. No matter how far and wide this family has spread — and it has gloriously spread around the world with no boundaries of ethnicity, color or tribe — it has roots. We should know and honor those roots.

Passengers exit the front of the station and instantly enter the lively heart of the city. People, street cars and bicycles abound. Crowds are joined at street car stops across a square. Most people do not bring their cars downtown. Ineke and Peter have a three-month parking pass for their quadrant of the city. They drive their car to the nearest point to the city center that their pass allows and park. Then, if picking someone up from the central station, they catch the street car to meet their visitors. If they are going for their own business, they go downtown on a bicycle or put a collapsible bike in the back seat of their car and ride it to their destination from where they stop within their parking permit area.

Ineke is a retired pastor who still works at a church without a pastor two days a week. Peter is a retired safety inspector. They live in the home of Peter's deceased parents in Amsterdam. A narrow park and canal are directly across the street. In expensive Amsterdam, Ineke and Peter could not afford the three-storey house on their own, so they turned the top two floors into a boarding house for students attending a nearby university. The Reinholds live on the main floor. They are happy with this arrangement because it allows

(far left) A Mennonite history tour of Utrecht.

(left) The Utrecht Mennonite Church constructed at a time in which the church could be visible from the street but was not allowed to look like a church.

(above) Ineke Reinhold outside the entrance to Amsterdam's Singel Church. The church was built behind the homes of three wealthy Mennonites, completely hidden from the street.

(opposite) The Krommenie church inside and out, restored as it was when it was built in 1703 to replace a church which had been burnt down in a 1702 fire that devastated the community.

(above) Sculpture by Annelies Soomers. (opposite, clockwise from top) Janneke Hoekstra, left, and Annelies Soomers, right. In Janneke's Krommenie backyard. Quilt by Janneke Hoekstra.

Watercolor painting by Annelies Soomers from her endangered creatures series.

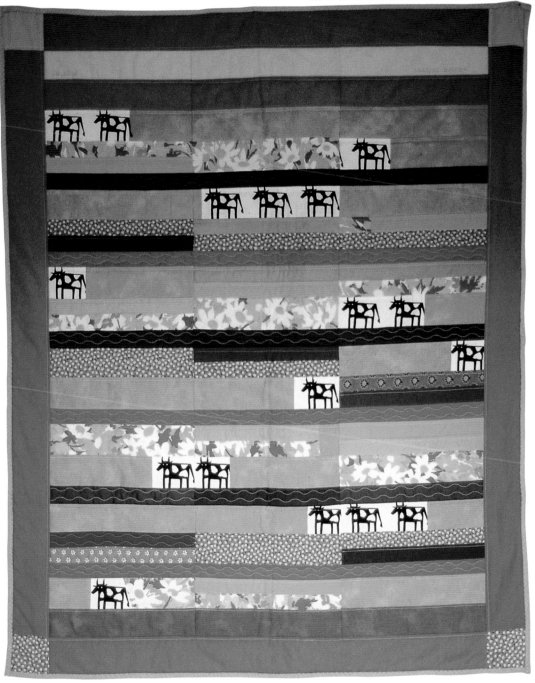

surface area: 1,919,440 sq. km.
capital: Jakarta
population: 219.9 million (2003)
language: Indonesian, 300 regional languages
major religion: Islam 87%, Christian 9% (some dispute this figure stating it is significantly higher), Hindu 2%, other 2%
literacy: 84%
life expectancy: 65 (men), 69 (women)
annual income per capita: US $690

United Nations Human Development Index: 112 out of 175 countries (2003)

Mennonite World Conference Member Churches

Name: Gereja Injili di Tanah Jawa
Local churches: 96
Members: 43,000

Name: Persatuan Gereja-Gereja Kristen Muria Indonesia
Local churches: 42
Members: 16,302

Name: Sinode Jemaat Kristen Indonesia
Local churches: 36
Members: 12,000

Gift Highlights: Lecturers in conflict resolution, counseling, economics and church history, missions and music gifts, administrative and craft skills, educational institutions, mission organizations, and social and economic programs

Indonesia

(this page) Fishers near Jepara on the island of Java. (opposite) Natural beauty along Java's volcanic spine near Salatiga. A single island with over 120 million people at the heart of a nation of more than 17,000 islands strung out over 3,000 kilometers. The most populous predominantly Muslim nation on earth.

family stories stories

Sudjojono was a trailblazer, a Communist, and an atheist. This deliberate thorn-in-the-side is considered to be one of the fathers of contemporary Indonesian art. He declared that Indonesian paintings did not have to be pretty pictures for colonialists. They could be about the real people, places and issues in his country.

When his son Abang was still a small boy, Sudjojono left and then divorced his first wife, Mia Bustam. Abang Rahino grew up not appreciating his father's achievements. He knew the man, not the legend — a man who had deserted his family for a selfish pursuit and another woman. The fact that the National Art Museum in Jakarta placed a bust of his father at its entrance was irrelevant to Abang.

As an adult Abang became a Christian. He decided he needed to join a church, but he did not want to simply go to the nearest one. He studied the confessions of faith of as many churches as he could find. It was the Mennonite confession that appealed to him. In a world of violence and intolerance he saw a confession that said members should actively pursue justice without violence. He interpreted the confession as saying that Mennonites believe in understanding, reconciliation and peace. Abang felt this was the best formula for healing in his troubled homeland. He saw the Christian churches which stood for confrontation with the majority Muslim population as provoking the extremist Muslims as opposed to accomplishing anything positive for God.

Sudjojono died in 1986. Eventually Abang became interested in what his father had achieved as an artist. An artist was also beginning to stir in Abang's soul. His growing interest in art and the role his father played in Indonesian art, plus the fact that Abang is a committed Mennonite Christian, made him a perfect principal contact for *In God's Image* in Indonesia.

Abang's father's name opens many cultural and artistic doors in Indonesia, especially in the massive, smog-enveloped political capital, Jakarta, and in the quaint and appealing cultural and artistic capital, Yogyakarta.

Most of the world has never heard of Yogyakarta. This city of about 500,000 is home to many universities and artists. It has a reputation as a tolerant and lovely place. The area's cultural, religious and historic importance goes back over a thousand years. Two significant ancient sites are nearby — Borobudur, with an astounding number of reliefs and statues, is the largest Buddhist temple complex in the world, and Prambanan, a Hindu site where a magnificent Javanese ballet now takes place nightly.

The arts are not only important in a traditional and historic sense in Yogyakarta. Indonesia's contemporary art, as can be readily seen in the city, is a window into a complex nation that is much more than simply the most populous predominantly Muslim nation on earth. Proof of the country's many

Abang Rahino with his mother, Mia Bustam, his sister and niece in Jakarta.

cultures and religious traditions is found in the art. The art verifies that this country cannot be categorized as a conservative Islamic monolith even though it is overwhelmingly Muslim. In discussion with several artists and the organizations supporting them — including the Asian Christian Art Association based in Yogyakarta — there is a desire among many within the artist community to be a positive force in Indonesia.

Abang, too, is now releasing the artist born within him. Fathered by an atheist in a predominantly Muslim land, a new Christian artist is evolving from within a middle-aged man. God's artistic gift to Abang has taken years along an unusual journey to be revealed. As an Anabaptist by choice, he is dedicated to using this belatedly discovered gift for God. His voice will join those of other artists working and praying for peace and reconciliation for their complex nation of more than 17,000 islands strung over 3,000 kilometers. Their task is immense, but the goal is worthy.

The vast majority of Muslims in Indonesia, according to Abang, are decent people, not fanatics. There are extremists and leaders who try to organize and provoke them against minority communities, with the hope of eventually bringing the reasonable majority to side with their intolerant views, but they are a minority.

An inspiring but potentially fragile story is unfolding in the small town of Sukodono. It is the story of a tiny minority community living as an example, true to its beliefs, not through confrontation but by fostering respect and earning a reputation as Christians by deed.

Sukodono is a quiet town near Jepara in Central Java, not far from the north coast. It is in the general area of the largest concentration of Mennonites in the country. Much of Java is unending humanity as similar looking cities, towns and villages ceaselessly fold into and out of one another. But there are areas of beautiful exception. Sukodono is a well treed community. Thin paved lanes seem always flanked by lush greenery. In the hazy dawn's milky light and the warm late afternoon sun's glow, gazing down any number of still, shadow-daubed streets is to view a poster of serenity.

Unemployment is low in this community. Nearly everyone is involved in furniture-making or, to a lesser extent, wood carving. With no exaggeration, all but a handful of homes in the community host a yard full of wooden, generally teak, furniture in various stages of development. Small furniture-making shops dot the residential districts, including one which employs a group of Mennonite young adults. In commercial areas virtually every business has something to do with furniture.

The Mennonite church is the only Christian congregation in this town. Well over 90% of Sukodono's population is Muslim. Taman Petra, his wife Ulis Tatik and their two young sons, Fillian Enggar Krisnada and Dwiokta Krisetya, live in Sukodono. Petra and Ulis come from longtime Mennonite families. Ulis first fell in love with Petra because of his love for the church and his dedication to serving the less privileged, both Christian and Muslim.

Petra is the lead Indonesian woodcarver contact for Ten Thousand Villages, the Mennonite-based fair trade chain of global South craft stores. He and his family live in a two-level residence with a workshop and rooms for apprentices on the main floor and Petra and Ulis' small home on the second. The open design of the upper floor allows for a constant flow of air, wonderfully refreshing in the tropical humidity. Apprentices are both Muslim and Christian young men who come from areas of high unemployment. Petra believes there is dignity in work and he hopes to release the apprentices from dignity-sapping lives of chronic unemployment. The apprentices stay for several months, learning the intricacies of woodcarving and how to organize their lives.

Scenes from the Mennonite church in Yogyakarta.

Sukodono's Mennonite church.

Petra does not care that he might be creating competition for the work he relies on for his income. His overriding concern is to be of Christian service to fellow Indonesians.

One handicapped former apprentice, Yanu, has become a part of Ulis and Petra's family. A year and a half earlier a pastor from Jepara told Ulis that he was trying to help a crippled young man, but he could not find anyone who was willing to take him in. Ulis immediately said they would accept him. Yanu joined the apprenticeship program. He completed it and returned to his village 100 kilometers away. He missed Petra, Ulis and especially their sons. Yanu returned to Sukodono and was accepted as part of their family.

Due to the Mennonites' honest reputation, and compassionate examples such as Petra's and Ulis', the two elected volunteer positions in Sukodono are both held by Mennonites. Petra holds one, the other is held by a businessman who defeated a Muslim candidate with a much higher level of education.

Mennonites in the wider area run many institutions of value to the entire community — schools, clinics, a hospital and other community services. Some former patients have joined Mennonite churches because they were treated so well during their stay in the Mennonite hospital in Kudus.

In 2001 Muslim extremists from outside were sent into Sukodono on at least two occasions. Their coming was likely orchestrated from distant Jakarta. They urged the local community to throw stones at the church. They tried to provoke Muslims to drive the Mennonites out of the town. Each time the local Muslims told the outsiders to leave; thus they, not the Mennonites, were driven out of Sukodono. This is a marvelous testament to a group of people who are working diligently to act as Christ in the community, to give aid to all, regardless of who they are, and to be people of integrity.

But it is still potentially a tenuous existence. Incidents either actually or perceived to be against Islam — even those carried out thousands of kilometers away by Western countries — could cause general suspicion to grow,

A young mother and her boy outside the Sukodono church. Children not being able to sit through a church service crosses many cultures.

giving the extremists a new issue or event on which to pin their hopes. Outside the radar of the world, perhaps next time the extremists will not be turned away.

Indonesia is an amazing, troubling, beautiful, confounding, inspiring, complex country. Mennonites such as Abang Rahino, Taman Petra and Ulis Tatik stir hope in this incredible mix. A belligerent Communist artist could not have known that he would father a dab of Christian hope in his beloved land — that his son would become a Mennonite by deliberate choice and use his emerging artistic gifts to spread the gospel of peace.

The Sukodono church nursery school. Ulis Tatik at church with her son Dwiokta Krisetya.

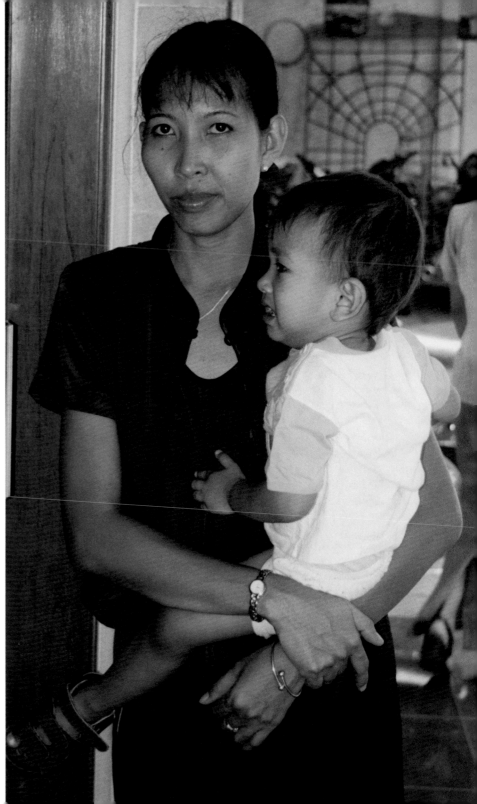

Yanu with Dwiokta. A loving home for a young man who had lost hope.

(opposite) An apprentice at work inside Taman Petra's workshop. (this page) Carving by Taman Petra, an apprentice at work and Taman Petra with his son, Dwiokta.

surface area: 377,835 sq. km.
capital: Tokyo
population: 127.6 million (2003)
language: Japanese
major religion: Shintoist, Buddhist, Christian
literacy: 99%
life expectancy: 78 (men), 85 (women)
annual income per capita: US $35,610

United Nations Human Development Index: 9 out of 175 countries (2003)

Mennonite World Conference Member Churches

Name: Nihon Kirisuto Keiteidan
Local churches: 7
Members: 171

Name: Nihon Menonaito Kirisuto Kyokai Kaigi
Local churches: 15
Members: 679

Name: Nihon Menonaito Kirisuto Kyokai Kyogikai
Local churches: 21
Members: 475

Name: Tokyo Chiku Menonaito Kyokai Rengo
Local churches: 5
Members: 95

Gift Highlights: Different skills, trainings and artistic abilities including computer expertise, gardening, flower arrangement, translation, as well as diverse musical gifts

Japan

family stories

The Japanese tradition is to admire delicate flowers rather than flamboyant ones — a mirror of the wish for humility and the desire not to stand out. In a land of technology-overload and a work pace that runs laps around those of some other places, order, peace and humility are cherished virtues. Ancient Shinto shrines, such as those near Kyoto, are simple, balanced, all things in place, in settings that invite feelings of peacefulness not far from the ubiquitous vending machines, neon signs and noise. Tokyo can feel overwhelmingly large, yet narrow "pedestrian only" lanes can create the feeling of a small, tranquil town.

The Honan-cho Mennonite Church is a short walk away from such a pleasant street. The street is lined with small shops and restaurants. People often retreat to restaurants to visit because most apartments in cramped Tokyo are very small. The stress from a long day in the city and on the commuter train eases with a stroll down the street.

A walk in many other districts of Tokyo induces other feelings. Akihabara, "electric town," includes the largest collection of electronic goods and parts in the world. One massive flea market-like building creates the sensation of being on a submarine while browsing in the cramped low-ceiling booths along narrow, jammed aisles. Harajuku is where the brashest of Tokyo's young gather to strut, pose, photograph each other and visit dressed in wild and bizarre outfits. The Shinjuku train station is one of the busiest in the world, once famous for having white-gloved staff who helped push and squeeze commuters onto packed trains. People spill out of the station into a riot of stores, flashing signs, full volume — sometimes screaming — advertisements on jumbo screens. Shinjuku is sensory overload. A short dash from Shinjuku is the massive Tokyo city hall, an ultra modern monument that cost so much to build, over one billion US dollars, the top floor observation deck is free of charge to try to salve angry citizens. The free view is staggering, an endless city with Mount Fuji visible in the distance on a clear day.

Tokyo includes the Honan-cho Mennonite Church somewhere in its vastness. A return to the pedestrian mall near the church calms the soul and makes the discovery of the tiny church somehow the final step towards a haven of peace. On Sundays the double doors of the church are opened. Flower pots are set up on either side of the doorway and in lines toward the narrow street, a garden pathway welcoming passers-by to come inside. A row of green flip flop slippers stand neatly in a line parallel

(opposite) Tenryuji Temple, part of the Ancient Kyoto UNESCO World Heritage Site.

(right) The heart of Shinjuku, one of the busiest areas of Tokyo.

to the small residential street. A stand filled with umbrellas in case it rains is on one side. As congregants reach the doorway they remove their shoes and put on a pair of slippers. Then they put their shoes in cubby holes just to the right of the entrance. A few extra pairs of slippers stay by the door for possible guests. The congregation is small, so they meet seated around a rectangle of tables, with Pastor Tanase at one end. He remains seated while preaching. When singing, the people all stand. Sermons are informal as a result of the small size of the congregation. There is an invitation for some interaction during the sermon. After the service Bibles are put away and lunch is brought out to be shared.

Japan's efficient train system, including the famous bullet trains, shuttle passengers about the country. The Japan rail network, according to Japan Rail, is the largest, most complicated, safest and most on-time in the world. A 1,000-kilometer trip from Fukuoka in the south to Tokyo takes only six hours. Hostesses in uniforms push trolleys filled with drinks and meals in wooden boxes. The boxes are separated into compartments, each with a different morsel that can be plucked out with chopsticks. Hostesses and conductors, no matter how much of a hurry they may be in, turn to face back into the car they are leaving and bow before swirling round and exiting.

Gen Tsuboi met me at Kyoto's spectacular central train station. Kyoto is not far from Japan's second city, Osaka, and is the cultural capital of the nation. Gen is an artist and interior designer. He lives with his wife Michiko and daughters Aino, Michino and Yokino not far from Kyoto. Gen has an office in the city. Michiko said the recent years of economic downturn in Japan have been good for their family. Gen has lost work and, therefore, is home more, and their family life is much better than before. There is a sense in their house that they are a family that likes each other and enjoys being together. Being together with the family is often a rarity in Japan, where most people work well beyond what is officially a full-time week.

Mari Iida enjoys visiting with her family. She is a single woman living not far from the Honan-cho church in Tokyo, where she is a member. She moved out of her parents' apartment and now rents a place a few blocks away. She enjoys the freedom that comes with living on her own, but she also appreciates living near her parents. She goes to visit them often, but they seldom eat together because their schedules rarely line-up at meal time.

The entrance to the Honan-cho Mennonite Church in a suburb of Tokyo. The service had already begun so only a scattering of slippers were left.

Mari lives on a typically narrow residential street with apartment buildings coming right to the curb. At intersections large convex mirrors allow approaching drivers to see around the tight crossings as they approach. Mari lives one floor above the street in a tiny apartment that is no more than a furnished hallway with a washroom. This is typical accommodation for single people in expensive Tokyo. Her kitchen is at one end and her bed with a headboard with shelves taking up the full width of the apartment at the other end. A low table, some shelves with a television and a computer are between the bed and kitchen. She has a closet and a tiny washroom to one side. She has no chairs. People sit on the floor around the low table to eat in the traditional Japanese manner.

Although she is a modern young woman, Mari is interested in knowing and preserving her culture. She has taken tea ceremony lessons for several years. Much more than the making of good tea is incorporated into the ceremony. For Mari it is a way of knowing and cherishing her culture, especially order, humility and peace, the values at the core of the ceremony.

Artist and teacher Kin Kawaguti, Mari's tea ceremony guide, has studied the tea ceremony for over 40 years. It is difficult for a non-Japanese to comprehend how someone could dedicate so much to something which seems so simple. Kin's home includes a special tea ceremony room — *chashitsu*. One wall is a floor-to-ceiling window. Her tiny yard fills the view with lush greenery, blocking out Tokyo just beyond. The other walls are traditional Japanese paper — *fusuma* — walls. The floor is covered in spare, beautiful, bamboo — *tatami* — mats with black cloth lines woven into them. Outside the door to the ceremony room there is a small stone wash basin built into the floor. This is where Mari begins her lesson.

She washes all the equipment she will use in the

Mari Iida, far right, in the Honan-cho church, worshipping and sharing lunch after the Sunday service.

In the southern city of Fukuoka.

ceremony and then enters the room bowing. Her teacher is on her knees watching and bowing slightly in return. There are different bows, both from the kneeling and standing position, signifying various levels of respect. Throughout the lesson the teacher and student react to each other following the rules of

(opposite) *Mari Iida on the street outside her apartment.*

(above) *Mari with a friend from church sharing dinner in Mari's small apartment.*

(right) *The work of a master ceramicist outside his gallery in Fukuoka.*

the ceremony. Nothing just happens. Every aspect is choreographed — from the washing of the pots, to the entrance into the room, to how the mats are negotiated according to the black lines woven into them, to the way the water ladle is held (differently at different stages), to the way the water is poured and the tea whisked, to the way accompanying sweets and the tea are served, and on and on. Everything must be done correctly and together with the meticulous layout and decoration of the room concentrates on grace, humility and beauty and points to peace, order and harmony. In the end a visitor to the ceremony receives some red bean sweets and milky pistachio colored green tea, but that is not why the ceremony has occurred.

Mari wants to know and guard her culture and traditions. She sees them as important in her life and for Japan. Her deep faith balances her spiritual life. She sees a search for peace and humility as an important part of being a Christian. She is dedicated to her culture as evidenced through her devotion to the tea ceremony. She is devoted to her faith as seen through her dedication to her church and the way she interacts with others. Mari is a follower of Christ in a Mennonite church, a believer in Christ as the Prince of all Peace.

Mari Iida at her tea ceremony lesson with her teacher Kin Kawaguti, who has studied the tea ceremony for over 40 years.

(opposite) A paper cut, kirie, artwork by Gen Tsuboi.

surface area: 35,980 sq. km.
capital: Taipei
population: 22.5 million (2002)
language: Standard Chinese, Taiwanese
major religion: Buddhist 4.86 million, Taoist 3.3 million, Protestant 422,000, Catholic 304,000
literacy: 94%
life expectancy: 72 (men), 78 (women)
annual income per capita: US $12,900

United Nations Human Development Index: 26 out of 175 countries (2003)
Taiwan, not formally recognized by the United Nations, is listed with Hong Kong as Hong Kong, China (SAR) in the HDI.

Mennonite World Conference Member Church

Name: Fellowship of Mennonite Churches in Taiwan
Local churches: 19
Members: 1,678

Gift Highlights: Medical ministry, other social programs, cross cultural mission

Taipei's claustrophobic congestion makes the Chiang Kai Shek Memorial Plaza even more impressive than it literally is. It is a massive open, concrete plaza flanked by the ornate National Theatre and National Concert Hall on each side and the Majestic Main Gate and the Chiang Kai Shek Memorial at opposite ends. In the evening parents bring their children to run and play in space and safety.

(opposite) Lover's Day is somewhat like Valentine's Day. Pastor Joshua Chang said he was not able to take his wife, Sophia Tsai, out to dinner but they did go for a walk holding hands. He said that the word "wife" literally means "the one whose hand you hold." I asked what "husband" means. There was a long pause. "Boss," he and Sophia, quipped in unison. They both laughed.

Taiwan

family stories

stories

Taiwan is an intriguing island. Is it or is it not a part of China? The majority of Taiwanese say it is not. Mainland China says it is.

The Mennonites of Taiwan are also intriguing. Insignificant in numbers but of significant influence, the community includes many professionals — businesspeople, doctors, teachers. Major social services in the east coast city of Hualien have been turned over by the government to be administered by the Mennonites. The New Dawn Center and the 800-bed modern Mennonite Hospital are among the well-known Mennonite institutions in the region.

Most visitors enter Taiwan through Taipei. Taipei is a huge, crowded city. It appears to be a metropolis of apartments and few houses, unless one heads to the surrounding hills, where large homes cling to steep hillsides. Despite the crush, Taipei is vibrant and inviting, with much to discover and enjoy. Outside the gleaming new parts of the city, street after street is an endless succession of similar nondescript buildings with no space between and innumerable neon signs in Chinese characters. At the pedestrian level there are countless small restaurants and shops, one after another along every side street — at least so it seems. Suddenly an exotic Buddhist and/or Taoist temple sprouts from a man-made canyon with a wild explosion of color, carvings and traditional architecture — a riot of delectable aesthetic filling squeezing out from a bland building sandwich.

The Fellowship of Mennonite Churches in Taiwan (FOMCIT) has its office and a guesthouse in Taipei's crowded jumble. The office is up a flight of stairs from the street. The guesthouse rooms are another flight up, past the apartment of Pastor Joshua Chang. His church, Sung-Chiang, meets near the FOMCIT office.

The Sung-Chiang church cannot be seen from the street. Expensive property and lack of land in Taipei means the church meets on the third floor of a condominium tower. From outside the building looks like any other apartment complex. The third floor elevator doors open to the foyer of the church.

In order to create the church all the condominiums on one floor were purchased and gutted. The largest area was converted into a lovely sanctuary. The sanctuary windows are each filled with glass paintings depicting biblical stories. Light from outside illuminates the semi-transparent artworks. They glow along one wall. There are several Sunday school rooms, a nursery and a kitchen. Simultaneous translation is available for English speakers through headsets supplied by the church. Sung-Chiang, thankfully, is air conditioned. Taiwan is oppressively hot and humid during summer. Every Sunday service is followed by a meal for the entire church supplied by a different woman each week.

Debbie Lin works in the FOMCIT office near the Sung-Chiang church. Debbie is a dedicated, efficient, self-effacing, gracious woman who is often the link between the conference and individuals, whether nationals or foreigners.

Not long ago Debbie fielded a call from a Mennonite art teacher from near Taichung. Lien-Nu Huang had a question. Soft-spoken Lien-Nu was not only an art teacher but also an accomplished artist. Her modesty meant that many people who knew her had no idea of

the scope of her artistic accomplishments. In 1992 one of her paintings was selected to be included in a prestigious international exhibition in Seoul, South Korea. The organizers were so impressed with the artwork that they asked if they could purchase it after the show ended. Lien-Nu said no and brought the artwork home.

Years later Lien-Nu began to think about the painting from the Korean exhibit. She felt God was telling her to donate it. But she could not think of an appropriate recipient. Finally Lien-Nu asked Debbie if she knew where she could bequeath the painting. Debbie, aware of the *In God's Image* project that led to this book and a corresponding touring exhibition, suggested she give the painting to *In God's Image*.

Lien-Nu and I met at a maternity and infant care center in a suburb of Taipei. The center was located in an apartment building. A row of flip flop sandals waited outside the door to the center. All visitors remove their shoes and slip on the sandals before entering. There was a waiting room, a nurses' station and a nursery immediately visible. The floors were gleaming, dark hardwood. Beyond were rooms, like hotel rooms, for the mothers at the center. The rooms were tiny but immaculate and richly appointed. Large windows offered a wonderful view as far as the smog would allow.

Before the rush of progress and the accompanying demand for more time than existed for most Taiwanese, tradition dictated that a new mother and her baby would be looked after by the mother-in-law for the first weeks or months. The new mother was to rest and be pampered. Now maternity and infant care centers are taking over that role. Mothers and newborns stay there with round-the-clock nursing care and their babies in the nursery separate from them, unless they want them in their rooms. The mothers rest there for a few weeks, as long as the family can afford the service.

Lien-Nu proudly presented her new grandson and the painting to be included in *In God's Image*.

Chich-Chun Yuan recently completed her Masters in Social Work at the Chinese Cultural University in Taipei. Earlier that same year a typhoon devastated the Ah Mei area along the east coast of Taiwan. The Ah Mei are one of Taiwan's nine aboriginal groups. Following her strong Anabaptist convictions, Chich-Chun felt that rather than look for work in her field after graduating she would go to the Ah Mei area and offer her services as a volunteer.

She took the train southeast from Taipei to the rugged east coast and then beyond Hualien. She found an area where clean-up work was underway, and she offered her help.

While working there she met Ah Mei artists dedicated to helping their people retain their culture, integrity and pride through their art. Chich-Chun had read about *In God's Image*. She called Debbie Lin and asked if I would be willing to meet with the Ah Mei artists near Hualien. As a Mennonite, she felt supporting the work and cause of those who are often on the fringes of mainstream society would be a Christ-like thing to do. As a result, Chich-Chun took Paulus Pan, a former Mennonite pastor, and me to meet Lin A Rong, the lead Ah Mei carver. He showed us around their busy workshop where a series of squat totems were being carved to line the roads of the area. After some discussion, a spectacular wood carving was commissioned for *In God's Image*.

It was raining in torrential waves the night before I left Taiwan. Despite the rain Debbie Lin left work for home on her scooter. We said good-bye as she departed. I went up to the guesthouse. Ten minutes later there was a knock on my door. Debbie was there, soaking wet and carrying a steaming bag in her hand. She had bought me supper, not wanting me to venture out in the bad weather. She wanted no payment and no thanks. She smiled, wished me God's blessings and headed back out into the storm on her scooter.

In my short time in Taiwan I met many Christians from Mennonite churches who were quiet, humble and determined examples of what it is to be a Christian in every part of one's life — at work, at home, with friends and strangers and in voluntary service simply for the good of others.

(opposite) At the famous Lungshan Temple, Taipei's oldest. The temple is both a religious and political symbol in Taiwan as the fledgling democracy movement held meetings at the temple during the days Taiwan moved away from dictatorship.

(right) A jumble of rooftops, old and new.

(far right) Debbie Lin with a street vendor from her church.

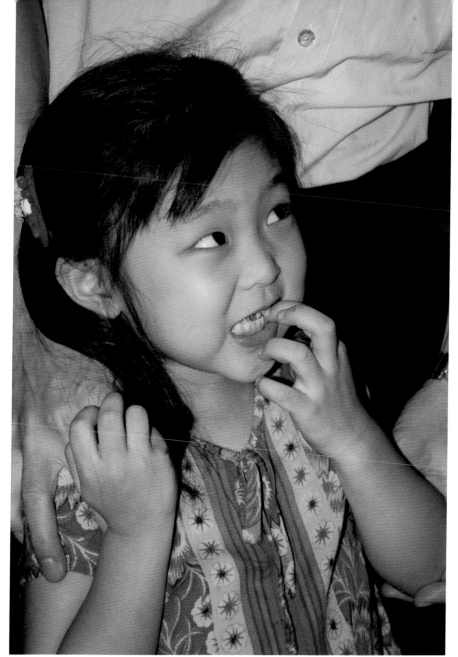

(opposite, clockwise from top left) Influential Mennonite businessman Paul Wang and his wife Polly at their home in the hills above Taipei. The New Dawn Center in Hualien. Government social services administered by Mennonites are run out of the center. Rice paddies on the outskirts of Hualien.

(this page) Some of the members of the Sung-Chiang congregation in Taipei.

(top right) Plastic surgeon Dr. George Wong and his wife Rebecca Lin in their Taipei apartment.

Eric Wang, along with his brother Paul, has significant business interests in Taiwan, China and the US. He is an avid art collector, especially of art from mainland China, and a good painter in his spare time.

(right) Painting donated to In God's Image by Lien-Nu Huang.

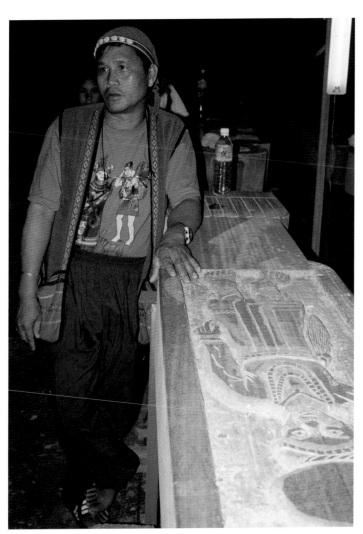

(clockwise from top left) Chich-Chun Yuan. On the morning this photograph was taken she was involved in a car accident. It was the fault of the other driver. He was older than Chich-Chun. To allow him to save face, she accepted only partial payment for the damage to her car and paid the rest out of her own pocket.

Ah Mei artist Lin A Rong. A carving based on Ah Mei stories by Lin A Rong.

Lien-Nu Huang.

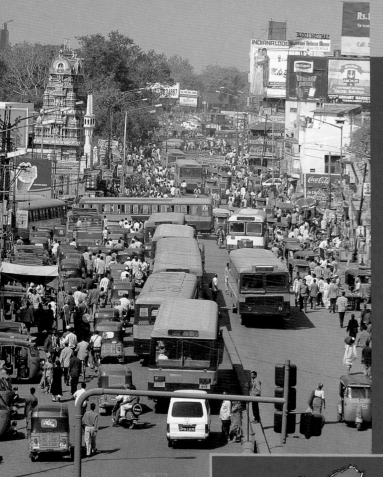

India

surface area: 3,287,590 sq. km.
capital: Delhi
population: 1 billion (2003)
language: Hindi, English and 17 other official languages
major religion: Hindu 82.6%, Islam 11.3%, Christian 2.4%, Sikh 2%, Buddhists 0.71%, Jains 0.48%
literacy: 52%
life expectancy: 63 (men), 65 (women)
annual income per capita: US $460

United Nations Human Development Index: 127 out of 175 countries (2003)

Mennonite World Conference Member Churches

Name: Bharatiya Jukta Christa Prachar Mandali
Local churches: 106
Members: 6,000
Name: Bhartiya General Conference Mennonite Church
Local churches: 26
Members: 7,000

Name: Bihar Mennonite Mandli
Local churches: 19
Members: 1,500

Name: Brethren in Christ Church Orissa
Local churches: 98
Members: 2,723

Name: Bharatiya Khristiya Mandali (Brethren in Christ Church Society)
Local churches: 55
Members: 3,297

Name: Conference of the Mennonite Brethren Churches in India
Local churches: 840
Members: 103,488

Name: Bharatiya Mennonite Church in India ki Pratinidhi Sabha (Mennonite Church in India)
Local churches: 19
Members: 3,437

Gift Highlights: Faith healers, computer technicians, social and health workers, agriculturalists, print and audio/video resources

family stories

family stories

My eyes opened with the break of dawn. Egrets, soft and white against the evolving blue sky crossed low overhead, moving with the daylight from one rice paddy to another. The flap of their wings was the only sound. The sky was our ceiling; its brightening was our alarm clock. This being the dry season we slept outdoors without fear of rain, and we were thus able to escape the oppressive heat inside the house.

Rufus G.K. stirred and noticed I was awake. "Would you like to go for a hike?" he asked.

The two of us left his mother's courtyard on the edge of Akuthotapally village. We passed the small whitewashed Mennonite Brethren church and a few pigs rummaging in a thicket. Women were already in front of their courtyard gates spreading a water-based mixture on the hard-packed dirt to keep the dust down for the day. They carried full buckets and scooped out the liquid by hand, spreading it evenly with a rhythmic, sweeping motion of their arm. We left the village behind and headed along a dusty road to a nearby small mountain — a jumbled pile of giant boulders stacked upwards to a towering point. We passed Rufus' father's grave. He had been the pastor in the local Mennonite Brethren church for 52 years before his death in 1993. We scrambled up the mountain. An enormous slab of rock formed a plateau about halfway up. Rufus said that every Easter morning the members of the church come to this spot overlooking the village to celebrate Christ's resurrection.

The view was spectacular. The ragged, arid landscape of Andhra Pradesh spread out forever. The house-size boulders around us were a warm, orange-tinged gold in the rising sunlight. The village was at our feet, gathered snug inside a necklace of vivid, green rice paddies. Rufus stood on the edge of a cliff gazing at the village. "I have a great burden for the people of my village."

Rufus is a school of fine arts graduate. He lives with his wife, Preshasthea, and his daughters Lisa, Nissy and Zailleh in Hyderabad, India's fifth largest city. He works as a photographer in the Information and Communications Center at Hyderabad's Agricultural University. But the desire to serve, especially the young, to bring them to Christ and to

(right) Shearamma in her courtyard in the village of Akuthotapally in Andhra Pradesh State. Many credit her for keeping the village church alive through the past decade.

(opposite) Secunderabad, Hyderabad's twin city. Hyderabad is a high tech center, the capital of Andhra Pradesh and the fifth largest city in the country. It is home to a large Muslim community within a Hindu majority.

help them grow in their faith causes him to return to his home village, Akuthotapally, often and to organize youth meetings and other events throughout areas of Andhra Pradesh where there are Mennonite Brethren churches.

Rufus follows in the dedicated footsteps of his father and is inspired by the passion for the church displayed by his mother, Shearamma. The Akuthotapally church has not had its own pastor since Rufus' father died. The salary is too low to attract anyone to this remote spot. Other area pastors sometimes come by to lead services. Mostly, Rufus' mother has taken it upon herself to make sure church members are visited and cared for, that they remain faithful and that they are prayed for. Prayer is central in the life of the Mennonites I met in Andhra Pradesh. Everywhere we went, in the day and at night, at homes and in churches, in alleys and on street corners, at the airport as I departed, we stopped, and whoever was with us formed a circle and we prayed.

Rufus has relatives spread throughout various communities around Akuthotapally and in Hyderabad. One day we were in a nearby larger town,

Amangal. The town is on the main highway and bustles with life. Many Lambani, a gypsy tribe whose distinctively and colorfully dressed women wear enough jewelry to each fill a bucket with what adorns them, pass through the town. A Hindu statue, exotic to western eyes, gazes peacefully over a chaotic small square, lost in the congestion. Away from the highway, off the small dirt road that leads to Akuthotapally a few of Rufus' siblings live in a community that includes Christians, Muslims and the majority Hindus. Here the well, just off the road, is the meeting point.

One of Rufus' brothers in Amangal is a local style doctor, not formally trained. Serious conditions are dealt with by doctors with medical school training. Rufus' brother handles a variety of less serious ailments. He lives in a

tiny house with his wife, two small sons and his wife's mentally handicapped younger brother. His wife is a teacher.

Another brother and his family live just up a slight hill past the well a short walk away. One of their teenage daughters has a condition that has caused her to lose much of the pigmentation in her skin. Her patchy skin color varies from very dark to pinkish white.

One day many of Rufus' relatives gathered in Amangal to go to Akuthotapally for a family get-together. We waited at the home of the doctor and teacher. Several women in gorgeous saris visited in the home until it was time to leave. I stood in the doorway. Two small boys and a puppy were playing at my feet. The dog suddenly darted through my legs. I swiveled to see where he was going. As I turned I saw the teenage niece with the skin condition standing within an arm's length of me. She was holding a white dove out towards me. Her mentally handicapped relative stood directly behind her, also looking at me.

In a few seconds the moment passed. The two young people moved on to do other things. The puppy returned to check on some live chickens wiggling in a burlap bag near my feet. The dove was placed into a cage. Chatting continued all around. That specific composition — the teenage girl, the handicapped young man, the dove, the open, peaceful and inviting expression on the girl's face — may never occur again in my life. But that moment will last in my mind's eye forever. It was as if God was making the point that *all* people are created in His image, that *all* people are equal in the eyes of God. The white dove, a Christian and oft-used Mennonite symbol, seemed the exclamation point.

The family moved on to Akuthotapally. En route we passed a small, ragtag group — three men, a couple of small children and a cow. Soon after arriving at Shearamma's the chickens in the bag met their demise. They were plucked and put into a pot. Almost everyone was involved in the preparation for a family feast.

In the evening, after everyone had departed, Rufus and I pulled Shearamma's and our cots outside in preparation for another night's sleep. Beyond the courtyard walls we heard a steady, monotone call coming closer. It continued in the same rhythm in Telugu and faded as the message bearer wandered past and on into the village.

"A circus is in town. Shall we go?" asked Rufus.

We found our way in the dark to the center of the small village, an area large enough for buses to turn round. It was surrounded by a few small shops. One bare light bulb illuminated what it could. Someone worked at getting a kerosene lantern lit. A couple of musicians sitting around him began to play. A cow wearing an ornate costume stood passively behind them. The small group we had passed along the road was the circus.

Over a period of at least an hour a crowd slowly formed and ringed the performers. Eventually a Hindu legend became the focal point of the circus performance. The musicians played on and the man who lit the lantern became the main performer. He called out the story while coaxing the cow into its trained moves. A reluctant volunteer was drafted. The lead performer encouraged the cow to chase the volunteer around the circle rimmed by the audience. The cow's horns whizzed past, a dim blur almost grazing the spectators. The volunteer fled before the cow. At one point he attempted to escape, was captured and returned to the fray. The performance ended with the volunteer lying prone in the square with the cow balancing a hoof, just touching but not pressing, on his face.

Small pleasures and customs continue in remote rural villages out of view of the world, away from the pulsating energy of India's cities which combine the newest of technology alongside the oldest of traditions. In Akuthotapally the old women still crouch in the shade, low against the cool courtyard walls to escape the searing heat. Small circuses still roam from village to village. The rhythm of life seems unchanged. Congregations of Christians move on in the rhythm.

(following pages) A weekly ritual at Shearamma's home in Akuthotapally. Her daughter-in-law and a friend prepare a mud based paint to spread on the ground in front of the walls of the compound. The friend then quickly and expertly sprinkles a design with powdery white sand — rangoli — onto the wet mud. Extra designs are added around the doorways.

Relatives prepare for a family feast at Shearamma's.

(clockwise from left) *The view looking out of the village from the roof of Shearamma's compound. During the sweltering months of the dry season many people sleep outside, on roofs or within their walled compounds.*

Rufus G.K. with his daughter Nissy.

Looking back at Akuthotapally from a nearby small mountain.

A painting with a traditional theme by R. Danny.

credits

Canada
designer/writer/photographer, Ray Dirks
editor, Larry Kehler
Ruth Maendel, Michino Tsuboi, Katie Dirks
Mennonite Heritage Centre: Alf Redekopp, Connie Wiebe
printer, Friesens, Altona, Manitoba
Very special thanks to John Wieler

Mennonite World Conference
foreword, Larry Miller
compiled "gifts" list for each country,
Pakisa Tshimika and Tim Lind
other assistance from Eleanor Miller,
Dothan Moyo, Ray Brubacher, Anna Sorguis

Map on page 6, 7 by Julie Kauffman, MCC, Akron, Pennsylvania

Sponsors
Frank and Agnes DeFehr
Herb and Erna Buller
Bill and Margaret Fast
Special thanks to Friesens, Altona

Brazil
Peter and Anne Pauls, Henrique Ens, Alfred Pauls, Geraldo Dyck, Liesbeth Vogt Hiebert, Peter Siemens, Konrad Dueck

Cuba
Felix Rafael Curbelo and Leyda Verde, Daniel Cabrera, José Ernesto Martin Torres, Maria Regla Reyes Coto, Jésus Lescano Peres and Maria E. Aguirre Calderon, Marcelino Mestre Elia and Martha Gonzalez Vega

Democratic Republic of Congo
Robert Neufeld, Mwaku Kinana, Rev. Ndunda
photographer, Mattieu Lelo

Ethiopia
Kenna Dula, Aster Wolde, Bedru Hussein, Girma Teklu, Kebede Bekere
Special acknowledgment to *Beyond our Prayers* by Nathan B. Hege, the history of the Meserete Kristos Church commissioned by the Ethiopian church.

France/Switzerland
Max and Astrid Wiedmer

India
Rufus Gurugulla, Gordon Nickel, Shearamma, Werner Kroeker

Indonesia
Abang Rahino, Marthen Tahun, Taman Petra, Ulis Tatik, Lilik Setiyanto

Japan
Mari Iida, Yoshiko Harada, Gen and Michiko Tsuboi, Sally Ito, Gerald Neufeld

the Netherlands
Ineke and Peter Reinhold, Annelies Soomers

Paraguay
Ewald and Katie Goetz, Ernesto and Elsa Unruh, Eduard Friesen, Melvin and Gudrun Warkentin, Hilde Amstutz

Taiwan
Debbie Lin, Paulus Pan, Joshua Chang, Chih-Chun Yuan, Paul Wang

Uruguay
Doris Haak, Günter Meckelburger, Hermann Woelke, Milka Rindzinski, Hugo Moreira, Maria Jésus Otero, Eva Maria Bachmann

United States
Doug and Joanne Ranck Dirks, Barbara and John Fast
photographer, Scott Jost

Zambia
Elijah Muchindu, Enock Shamapani, Leonard Hamasele, Abert Seemani, Daniel and Sophia Seemani

Zimbabwe
Ronald Lizwe and Su Moyo, Dothan and Sigqibile Moyo, Rodger Moyo, Voti Thebe

In God's Image exhibition sponsors; principal among them the DeFehr Foundation, Mennonite Central Committee, Mennonite Central Committee Canada, Paul and Polly Wang, Bill and Margaret Fast, Neil and Herta Janzen

Please forgive us for those who have been missed. Many more than listed above have helped and donated to the exhibition. All contributions were valuable.

Special thanks to Ronald Lizwe and Su Moyo and the street children of Emthunzini Wethemba House in Bulawayo, Zimbabwe. You gave me a peaceful and inspiring place to work at just the right time.   *Ray Dirks*

In God's Image: A Global Anabaptist Family
THE EXHIBITION

An exhibition of the art and the daily life photographs from the 17 countries featured in this book is available for touring. It includes over 100 pieces of art and 48 photo panels. There simply is no other introduction to the worldwide Anabaptist family anything like this exhibition. *In God's Image* opened at the National Gallery of Zimbabwe in Bulawayo in July 2003 and from there it went to the Assembly Gathered of Mennonite World Conference in the same city in August 2003. One Zimbabwean observer at the National Gallery opening stated, "I feel like I have just taken a trip around the world visiting friends along the way." If interested in the exhibition, please, contact Ray Dirks at rdirks@mennonitechurch.ca or (204) 888-6781. Mailing address: Mennonite Heritage Centre Gallery, 600 Shaftesbury Blvd., Winnipeg, MB Canada R3P 0M4.

Mennonite World Conference

Mennonite World Conference (MWC) is a global community of Christian churches who trace their beginning to the 16th-century Radical Reformation in Europe, particularly to the Anabaptist movement. Today, nearly 1,300,000 believers belong to the Anabaptist-related family of faith; at least 61 per cent are African, Asian or Latin American. For more information, contact Mennonite World Conference at info@mwc-cmm.org or 8 rue du Fossé des Treize, 67000 Strasbourg, France. Or visit MWC at www.mwc-cmm.org.

Mennonite Heritage Centre Gallery
Winnipeg, Canada

This book comes out of an exhibition of the same name based in the Mennonite Heritage Centre Gallery (MHCGallery). The gallery is owned by Mennonite Church Canada and is situated on the campus of Canadian Mennonite University in Winnipeg. It is an institution within a church community that says art can be relevant and artists are God gifted. Local artists and ones from across Canada are featured. It also works with artists from the global South on a scale unmatched in Canada. Exhibitions from Cuba, Sudan and Indonesia have toured in Canada and the US, including New York City. The MHCGallery works with artists from recently arrived immigrant and refugee communities in Canada and involves their community cultural groups in its programming. These have included artists and performers from Indonesia, Afghanistan, Sudan, Ethiopia, Eritrea, Uganda, Ghana, Cuba, the Caribbean and other countries and regions. The Gallery operates a program out of a Winnipeg inner city high school working with English as a Second Language students, most of whom are newly arrived refugees, using art as a way to help them feel proud of who they are and where they come from thus helping them to integrate into Canadian society more easily.

Gallery curator Ray Dirks has worked with artists from 30 countries and has had exhibitions of his own art in Canada, the USA, Ethiopia and Cuba. In 2002 he was a Research Fellow at Yale University and Artist-in-Residence at the Overseas Ministries Study Center, both in New Haven, Connecticut.

The Gallery is wholly supported through tax deductible donations. Would you like to help? For more information contact curator Ray Dirks at (204) 888-6781 or rdirks@mennonitechurch.ca.